Advance praise for Y

"*Stress is a natural and pervasive part of life.* You Can Heal Your Child *explains the effects of stress on children in a unique and important way. Anyone who reads this book will feel empowered by both its hopeful message and clear direction on what we, as parents, can do to ensure our children's success.*"

~ Melinda Bossenmeyer, Ed.D.
Retired Principal and Administrator,
Founder of Peaceful Playgrounds

Dr. Melrose has a strong understanding of children. She understands their challenges and outlines them well. You Can Heal Your Child *is a book I highly recommend for those who want to prevent the effects of stress or trauma in children or for those who have children already stressed or traumatized.*

~ Elizabeth Bennett
author of *Peer Abuse Know More! Bullying From a Psychological Perspective*

"*This book is a life saver, one that every parent should read.*"

~ Britt Michaelian, M.A.
author of the bestseller *Secrets of the Safety Goddess: A Modern Safety Guide for Busy Parents* and Co-Founder of Responsible Teachers ("Turning Educators into Entrepreneurs to Give Children the Well-Rounded Education they Deserve" at responsibleteachers.com)

you can heal your child

A guide for parents of misdiagnosed, stressed, traumatized, and otherwise misunderstood children

Regalena Melrose, Ph.D.

author of *Why Students Underachieve: What Educators and Parents Can Do about It*

60 Seconds Press
Long Beach, California

ISBN-13: 978-0-615-88569-8
ISBN-10: 0-615-88569-1
Library of Congress Control Number: 2009924882

Printed in the United States of America

You Can Heal Your Child 2009

Published by:
60 Seconds Press
3519 East Second Street
Long Beach, CA 90803
drmelrose.com

Editor & Proofreader: Kenneth W. Owens, Psy.D.
Title & Guidance: Alicia Dunams
Cover & Layout: Paul McBride Mahan
Printer: CreateSpace

Table of Contents

for Jules

Acknowledgements

My almost four-year-old son reminds me often that whatever I may get wrong in a moment of stress or overwhelm, I can always repair, with my heart in the right place, by listening, not defending, by just hearing him and letting his feelings and perceptions be real. Thank you, Jules, for helping me experience myself as a bigger person than I ever thought possible. I heal with you, and because of that my work is informed by you in ways you may never know.

To my dear, dear friends, all of you and you know who you are. I am blessed to have so many of you and I need you every one. Thank you for holding me up.

To all those who's invaluable work has come before me. You have enlightened me, inspired me, taught me everything I know, and give me the courage to keep going.

To my students, for teaching me as much if not more than I have the privilege of passing on to you. Your youth and exuberance are medicine to me now.

Finally, to my clients, I am in awe of your courage, the depth of your spirit, and more than honored that you share your stories with me. Brothers T. and T., a special thanks to you for wanting your lives to be an inspiration to others. My work and this book are better off because of you.

Introduction

We are in the middle of an economic crisis. If we haven't lost our job, we have lost income, money on our investments, our retirement, or our home. The stress that these financial difficulties place on us can be devastating to our ability to be "here and now," fully present in our life, appreciating and enjoying what is left, and more importantly, parenting our children in a healthy way.

Many of our children are struggling too, whether they are twenty-three, thirteen, or three. Their lives aren't any less stressful than ours. They go from the ever increasing academic and social demands of school to activities, practices, clubs, rehearsals, work, dad's house, mom's house, feeling the same pressures we do. They are presented daily with the expectation to do better, be better, and get to the next level. Many children experience stress that goes beyond what we would ordinarily imagine or expect for their age. Some live in impoverished, sometimes dangerous communities. Others live in homes with a family member who is ill or abusing drugs or alcohol. Some have been in and out of hospitals trying to survive their own chronic illness. Others still, try to cope with being different somehow, in a way that makes them a target for abuse. They experience bullying, racism, homophobia, and other forms of hatred and maltreatment at the hands of peers and adults, including siblings and caregivers.

In addition to their own daily pressures, our children soak up the stress of the adults around them like a sponge. They feel what we are feeling. They are especially tuned in to us as parents more than we realize. They see and hear, not what we are trying to portray, but what is really going on. *The good news is that if we are managing our stress well, engaging in all the things that help us feel balanced and connected, grounded and whole, our children pick up on what is working in our lives and are soothed by their experience of us.*

This book addresses what we can do as parents to help our children thrive in the face of these uncertain times, in spite of the pressures that are a normal part of being alive. The book addresses both the problem of ongoing (referred to in studies as "chronic") stress and traumatic stress. Traumatic stress is the result of our children experiencing events that are extraordinarily frightening or difficult. Though you may not believe your child with difficulties has ever experienced a trauma, or that your healthy child ever will, statistics overwhelmingly indicate that, as long as we are living on this unpredictable and often dangerous planet, it is likely that they have or they will.

Traumatic experiences are not, as we would like to believe, outside the range of possibilities for our children. They are not so uncommon that they "couldn't possibly happen to anyone we know," let alone to someone we love so much. Dismissing trauma as the possible source of our children's difficulties and lack of hoped-for success is one of the most costly mistakes we can make. Doing so can prevent us from finding the most effective solutions and has, in many cases, contributed to the continuation of harmful interventions such as the medication or overmedication of children as young as three years of age. When hasty conclusions are drawn without consideration for our child's entire history and experiences, unnecessary suffering is prolonged for all of us.

Neuroscience involves the study of the brain. Because the brain mediates all of learning and behavior, there are a few basic neuroscientific facts that are important for us to know if we want to understand how it is that our children develop some of the problems they do. For instance, when we learn how our child's brain develops, functions and is affected by stress and trauma, we discover what interventions work best and why. Better still, we realize how to prevent problems from ever developing in the first place.

When parents come to see me, they have questions and concerns about how and why their child is having difficulty with learning or behavior. This book serves to answer those questions and concerns so that whole families - parents *and* children - will know precisely what to do to get through tough times and any other challenge that may come their way.

1
What's Wrong with My Child?

Kim

On the first day of school one year, a mother came to visit me at my office on the campus of a large neighborhood school. She shared with me the concerns she had for her daughter, Kim, who, at fifteen years of age, was having night terrors that had increased in intensity over the years. In fact, during the night terrors Kim became "a wild animal, on the attack," leaving her mother baffled by such alarming behaviors.

Kim had once done very well in school, but now was described by her mother as an underachiever. She was intelligent and could do anything she put her mind to, but "it's like she's given up and doesn't care. She often says apathetically, 'I forgot,' while explaining why she doesn't bring home her homework or finish an assignment. Even when she does finish an assignment, she'll forget to turn it in! It's beyond frustrating." Kim's grades were dismal and her future at risk. Still, after we met I knew, just as her mother did, that she could be a star student.

Kim's mother and I started at the beginning of her daughter's story. With patience, courage, and an open mind, she shared important details of Kim's life that helped us understand what was happening and why. She recalled the time Kim was eighteen months old and had developed a contagious virus for which she required quarantine in the hospital. The mother remembered that Kim's room had to be kept dark at all times, that neither she nor her husband (Kim's father) could stay with her. After several days, when she was able to come home again, Kim seemed different to her mother in some way, but not in a way she could pinpoint or explain. Maybe she was "quieter," the mother thought. "Less engaged and engaging." She couldn't quite articulate the change, but she felt it.

As most of us in that situation might have done, Kim's mother simply hoped that with time the girl she knew before the hospital stay would resurface and everything would be fine, and for the most part, that is what happened. The exception, of course, was the development of the night terrors that began approximately eighteen months after the hospitalization. While Kim seemed over time to get back to normal during her waking hours, the night terrors only got worse. Could the two experiences be related?

Sam

A divorced father brought his nine-year-old son, Sam, to see me in private practice because of the boy's "immaturity." He often "whined, cried easily, and wet his pants during the day." While the family worked with a pediatrician to rule out a medical condition that might explain the accidents, it was Sam's whining behavior that was the most bothersome to the dad because of its frequency and intensity given the boy's age.

After working with the family for a few weeks, I asked Sam and his father how much whining had taken place since our last visit. They reported that it had improved remarkably and that there had been no accidents that week either. When I asked what they attributed the improvement to, Sam answered quickly and matter-of-factly, "I haven't been in school this week." (It was the school's winter break.) This simple yet clear and determined answer helped us to understand the cause of Sam's behavior.

During a family session, together with his older sister corroborating, Sam recalled being bullied from the time he entered Kindergarten. He was teased, taunted, threatened, and pushed around in a way that always seemed to be minimized by the adults he reported it to. Instead of adults taking the incidents seriously and intervening to be sure they stopped, they cautioned the boy not to be a "tattle tale," and to learn to "toughen up." "Kids can be cruel," he was told. "You need to grow a thick skin."

In that same family session, when Sam's father asked him if he felt his experiences with the "mean kids" at school were more like teasing, he cut his father off and asserted, "What happens to me at school is not teasing! It's bullying!" Sam understood the difference and was taking a stand against it finally letting his father know that he wanted him to stop telling him to "take it like a man."

Sam's father was confused. "I don't get it. He says he doesn't whine when he is in school, where the problem is, and yet whines at home where he's loved."

"Exactly," I explained. "At school, he does his best to hold himself together and put up a good front so that he isn't bullied even more for appearing weak or hurt. That takes a lot of energy. Believe me. It is only when he feels safer that he can finally allow himself to feel how much

pain he is in, how insecure and afraid he truly is. That is when he can let go and exhibit the behaviors that are both a release of what he suppresses all day as well as his cry for help."

As parents we often look back on our own childhood experiences to try to understand and often to normalize what our children are going through. We say things like, "I was teased in school, or 'bullied,' if that's what they're calling it these days, and it never bothered me. I'm fine!" But are we fine? Were we fine then? Or did we learn to cope with whatever hurt us or scared us, by eating too much or too little, smoking, drinking, taking drugs, or engaging in some other behavior that helped numb, or at least distract, us from the pain. If we were able to find healthy ways of coping like sports, the arts, or being in nature, then we grew up at a time when those very important resources were more readily available and encouraged. Many children today don't have the same opportunities to play outside. As parents we're afraid to let our children out of our sight. In school, they have less physical education, recess time, and the arts, and at home, they have more time alone in front of a computer, television screen, or video game.

Our culture has changed. We are learning more and more about the genuine effects of some of the dangers we all faced growing up. We now have a better understanding of how the brain can be changed by the very real events, experiences, and circumstances that we lived when we were young and that many of our children are living now.

This book is not about what we wish was true for our family and our children or what we hoped our children's lives would be like when we imagined having them. This book is about what is *really* going on, what our children are really exposed to, affected by, and changed because of.

I've learned that the answer to the question, "What's Wrong with My Child?" often comes from the courage to consider the genuine effects of events we had hoped were insignificant. We can no longer afford to underestimate the potential links between the events and circumstances of our children's lives and their emotions, their learning, and their behavior. We can no longer afford to make assumptions about our children's experiences based upon our own. We must instead allow ourselves to see and accept the *reality* of *their* life and world, and how they are holding up as a consequence.

2
What are the Real Events of Our Children's Lives?

While many of our children's experiences are healthy and nurturing, some can be frightening, threatening, even devastating to them. Children living the same set of circumstances or events may experience them in an entirely different way. What one may find thrilling, invigorating, or exciting - a carnival ride, for example - another may find overwhelming or terrifying. The fact that the same event can have different effects for different children is why we mustn't make comparisons to try to determine what should be more or less stressful or traumatic for all. Making comparisons is how we minimize, negate, or invalidate our children's perceptions. What is important for us to notice and care about is the impact on *our* child of what happened or is happening still.

Let us consider some of what our children experience:

- hospitalizations, surgeries, medical & dental procedures
- bullying & other forms of peer abuse including
  acts & words of racism or homophobia
- exposure, often prolonged, to violent, scary, even terrifying
  media, including action and/or horror films as well as the news
- near death experiences such as very high fevers, almost drowning
  [even in the bathtub], suffocating, burning, accidental
  poisoning, or exposure to extremes in temperature

- economic hardship including the sudden loss of an income or home, chronic financial stress, poverty, hunger, or homelessness
- chronic disease, pain or serious illness in the child or parent
- sudden death or loss of a loved one
- marital discord, separation, divorce, domestic violence
- substance abuse on the part of a caregiver
- emotional, verbal, physical or sexual abuse from anyone the child knows, including siblings
- parental abandonment or neglect
- fetal distress (high levels of stress during pregnancy and/or birth)
- birth complications
- general anesthesia
- accidents, major or minor, involving cars, bicycles, et cetera
- falls & injuries
- prolonged immobilization from casting or splinting
- being threatened, attacked or bitten by an animal
- being lost, at the mall or in a strange neighborhood, for example
- exposure to community violence, such as witnessing or experiencing an act of violence in school or in the neighborhood
- transience, immigration, culture shock

Of course not every child who experiences one or more of these events becomes traumatized. In fact, there are two factors that distinguish children who become traumatized from those who do not:

1. Previous experiences of extreme stress or trauma;
2. Availability of resources.

Having a history of stressful or traumatic incidents can create a vulnerability or sensitivity in our child's nervous system turning any additional event, however alarming or threatening, into the "straw that broke the camel's back." This is because there is a cumulative effect of stress and trauma on the nervous system over time.

The availability of resources, however, can serve to buffer the potential negative effects of stress and trauma. Resilience is fostered by the availability of resources before, during, or after an event.

These two distinguishing factors are related because children who don't have a significant history of stress or trauma often have more resources available to them, such as the valuable *internal* resource of a nervous system that is biologically better equipped to navigate through frightening events. This is often the healthy product of an early development that wasn't plagued by chronic stress or debilitating incident. Children do better after a crisis when they have *external* resources available to them as well, such as a safe and stable family to go home to, close friends they can rely upon to help them cope, and recognition for talents and abilities that serve as outlets.

3
How Can Chronic Stress and Trauma Affect My Child?

Roy

When I met with eleven-year-old Roy's father and step-mother, they described him as "totally normal in school," in fact, "doing great in school," but "absent-minded." They were perplexed by the degree to which he was "totally unaware of his surroundings" and was forgetful. They wondered if he was forgetting things on purpose. They described Roy as shy and withdrawn with only one friend, and said he often complained, especially at night when going to bed, of a sore belly, headaches, and feeling itchy. Roy's parents reported that he had a "nervous tic." He was "always adjusting the top of his boxers." They said he needed "constant attention," was "clingy" and often talked "like a baby."

Roy's parents explained that when Roy was seven years old, his mother suddenly died while at work of a massive coronary. Essentially, from Roy's perspective, his mother went to work one day and never came home. Seven days before she died, Roy became ill and the family was under an inordinate amount of stress trying to figure out what was wrong. The father stated that he believed that Roy "carries with him" the thought that his mother's death was his fault.

Once Roy's father felt strong enough to do so, he put Roy, along with his younger brother, into bereavement counseling, but while his brother took to the program well and seemed to benefit from it, Roy did not.

The father didn't know what else to do, so he simply loved his boys the best way he knew how and hoped they would heal on their own. He remarried when Roy was nine and they got on with their lives, or so he thought. It became clearer to him over the years, however, that Roy was not getting on with his life. Rather, "he seemed stuck."

Roy's father described his son perfectly. Getting "stuck" in time inside our body and mind is exactly what can happen to our children after they experience an event that is terrifying or threatening to them. Again, it doesn't matter whether or not someone else would experience the same event as terrifying. It doesn't even matter whether the event that terrified the child was real or not. Children can get "stuck," as Roy's father put it, after any event - real or *perceived* - that is terrifying or threatening *to them*.

Remember, not everyone who goes through what some may call a "tough time, a crisis, or stressful period" becomes stuck. Depending upon how many resources are available before, during, or after the event, as well as whether or not the child has gone through other crises in the past, some do well in the face of extreme stress and carry on without any noticeable sign of what they went through. Others, however, *even if at first they seem all right*, later develop signs and symptoms that something is not the same.

The effects of chronic stress and trauma are not always noticeable immediately following the event(s) that caused them. An early fall that causes shock or injury may produce no obvious problems at first. It may not be until years later, until another frightening event occurs that the effects of a previous incident begin to show. Dr. Peter Levine (1997), a leading expert on the healing of trauma, wrote in his book, "Waking the Tiger: Healing Trauma," that "symptoms can remain dormant, accumulating over years or even decades. Then, during a stressful period, or as a result of another incident, they can show up without warning."

As weeks, months, and years pass, children who seemed "just fine" immediately after a crisis may begin to struggle with their sleeping patterns, eating patterns, level of concentration, and/or ability to focus and be in the "here and now." Some may become more agitated, more easily upset, and more difficult to soothe. They may report a sore tummy, headaches, or pain in their limbs. Others may report nightmares, difficulty remembering, and "jitteriness" inside that will not go away. Children who experience extreme stress or trauma may develop a sense that something bad is going to happen and they need to be ready for it.

Sofie

Thirteen-year-old Sofie was being treated for ADHD with medication but she was not getting better. In fact, she was getting worse. I met her after a long period of different medication trials that only seemed to exacerbate her problematic behaviors. Stimulant medications and antidepressants were tried and abandoned as they each failed to bring about the behavior change that everyone hoped for. Meanwhile, I worked with Sofie and her family to try to understand why it was that so many dif-

ferent medications often effective with children with ADHD were not working for Sofie.

After collecting a detailed developmental history, it became clear that Sofie was not ADHD at all. It was not hyperactivity she was displaying, but hypervigilance. The source of her inattentiveness was not the neurological condition of ADHD but the experiential condition of anxiety – the result of having been in a car accident that not only caused her own injury but left her father's unconscious body mangled in front of her. Sofie's symptoms of nightmares and intrusive thoughts about the event were consistent with what some experts call a "post-traumatic stress response" – the body's natural way of responding to an unnatural event. The source of Sofie's symptoms was trauma making the use of medication problematic to the healing process.

In a similar case I worked on many years ago as an intern, I met with my supervisor and two psychiatrists to urge them to reconsider their treatment of a boy that was not ADHD but traumatized. Very quickly the psychiatrists insisted that they treated symptoms and symptoms only. The boy presented as someone who was "hyperactive," they said, and therefore needed to be treated for that cluster of symptoms specifically. Because they did not consider the source of the boy's behaviors, the symptoms were misunderstood. He continued to receive medication for the wrong illness and before long became psychotic.

It is now well known that Post-Traumatic Stress Disorder (PTSD), the real source of the boy's difficulties, when left untreated, can lead to psychosis over time. Progression of the disorder is avoidable, however, when we are diagnostically accurate and appropriately tailor our treatment to manage the specific symptoms involved. In the case I was involved with as an intern, what needed to be intervened with was ignored, at great cost to the boy and his family.

The psychiatrists adopted a common orientation of concern for what was *presently* being observed and reported. In fact, that is the most valuable place from which to operate. Children with problems are experiencing difficulty in the present and need to be intervened with in the present. There is a way to do this, however, without ignoring or minimizing important historical events.

My conversation as an intern with the psychiatrists occurred before we knew as much as we do now about stress and trauma in children. We have begun to realize, through the help of recent research, that there is an important difference between hyperactivity, hypervigilance, and anxiety. We are starting to recognize that while these symptoms can appear remarkably similar in children they are in fact very different in origin. In order to make important distinctions between similarly-looking symptoms we must assess history thoroughly by asking specific questions about potentially stressful or traumatic experiences throughout development from the first moments of life. When we fail to do so, grave mistakes in both diagnoses and treatments are possible.

The medication of our children is one treatment that serves as a case in point. Children who are chronically stressed or who have been traumatized are too often misdiagnosed as ADHD and, as a consequence, are not helped but harmed by stimulant medication. Likewise, they are misdiagnosed as Bipolar because they often exhibit a volatile nervous system. They display emotional swings from elevated states of happiness and robust energy to irritability, frustration, aggression, and exhaustion. When they are misdiagnosed as Bipolar and treated as such, they are not helped but harmed by the medications typically prescribed.

Martin

I met with ten-year-old Martin's very concerned mother who was "willing to do anything" to help her son. When I met with her she stated that the main reason she needed help for Martin was his "lack of concentration in class." She went on to say that "he's so bad." He "tips his desk, throws his paper during silent reading, cannot study on his own, and always has to have someone with him." The mother said that she wanted him tested for being "extra active," stating that at home, Martin is "fidgety, can't sit still, argues over homework, and ends up in tears."

Given Martin's symptoms, a natural assumption would be that he had a classic neurological condition readily helped by psycho-stimulant medication. However, after considering Martin's history, we developed a much richer, deeper, and more comprehensive understanding of what was really going on. Martin had a kidney disease for which, since the age of five, multiple hospitalizations and surgeries were necessary. Many of the times Martin needed to be in the hospital for extended stays his mother could not be with him. She was a single parent and needed to be at work.

One can only imagine how frightened Martin must have been, a young boy left with strangers at a hospital to be probed, prodded, needled, restrained in some cases, and operated on. Martin's mother stated that since the time of his last hospitalization – and "that one was really bad" – Martin began flinching anytime someone who was physically close to him moved. She was extremely concerned at the time of our meeting because his once good grades had dropped.

Children like Martin are not understood when we ignore their history – the source of their difficulties – and simply treat their current symptoms. Medicating his "extra active" behaviors with the typical medications used for such symptoms would have been throwing gasoline on a fire.

Children like Martin are also not helped when we minimize their experience with statements like, "Kids are resilient. He'll be fine. He'll get over it with time." Rather than jumping to conclusions that may or may not be accurate, or making assumptions, we must make every effort to know how our child is really doing.

Furthermore, let us be aware that our verbal counsel is often ineffective with chronically stressed or traumatized children because the part of their brain that processes language is less available to them (more on this in the chapters ahead). We believe that if we take our children aside, talk with them in a way that elicits their description not only of the problem but also the solution we will see improvement because we took time to counsel them. Our logical mind is hoping to intervene effectively with children at a logical or cognitive level because that not only "makes sense," it is also our comfortable way of working through problems.

We are more than just our cognitive mind, however, and so are our children. We are mind *and* body. Stress and trauma are experienced by both mind *and* body. Events that are stressful or traumatic elicit powerful, instinctual responses in the body that set in motion the problematic behaviors we want to see improved. We want to believe our children have what it takes to control the effects of their overwhelming experiences by harnessing their cognitive mind, yet how many times in our own lives have we said we would never do something again, only to end up doing exactly what we said we wouldn't – over and over and over again? We have to stop replacing reality with what we wish was true. When it comes to powerful instinctual energy alive and well inside of us as well as our children, none of us has absolute control. Despite our good intentions and best efforts, when we ignore a problem's origin and intervene with the mind and not the body, our stressed and traumatized children get worse, not better.

When we ask the question, "How Can Chronic Stress and Trauma Affect My Child?" let us first understand and accept that they can. Chronic stress and trauma can and do affect our children in more ways than we have imagined. Potential learning, emotional, and behavioral problems can be prevented, however, and intervened with successfully when we are fully informed and thus less susceptible to ineffective solutions.

You Can Heal Your Child

4
How Can I Tell if My Child has been Traumatized?

There are numerous signs and symptoms that let us know when our child has been traumatized. As we review these signs and symptoms, it will become apparent that many of them are also part of other more commonly diagnosed problems, such as ADHD, Bipolar Disorder, anxiety disorders and depression. It is important to remember, however, that traumatized children display behaviors that are *natural* responses to unnatural events and circumstances. In many cases, the natural responses of these children do not constitute a "disorder" at all.

Misinterpreting children's behavior has become a serious problem in the fields of medicine, mental health, and education. As illustrated by the case example of Sofie as well as the boy I tried to help as an intern, children are being misdiagnosed and prescribed ineffective medications that often do not work because the conceptualization of the problem is wrong. It is my hope that with more parents learning about stress and trauma and the impact these conditions have on children's functioning at home and at school, we will stop the misdiagnoses and overmedication of too many of our children.

Once chronically stressed or traumatized, two different patterns of responding to the environment emerge. Some children appear hyper, aggressive, or highly irritable – an overaroused-looking pattern – while other children look shut down, spacey, or withdrawn – an underaroused-looking pattern. Whether overaroused or underaroused, the key to understanding chronically stressed or traumatized children is to know that their nervous system is unregulated and out of balance. It is revved high and wound tight.

When comparing these two response patterns, overarousal often looks like children have lost control of themselves. Picture the child who is constantly getting up out of his seat, trying to get involved in other people's business, putting his hands and feet where they are not wanted. Consider the child who looks for fights, using his body and face to intimidate, threaten and provoke. Think of the child who looks at people suspiciously and often complains that people are looking at him funny, trying to start a fight. These are the children who are overaroused, who get noticed, and who are more obviously stressed or traumatized.

Alternatively, think of the child who has given up. The one who does not seem to try anymore, who sits at her desk claiming she is bored, or does not care, or nothing matters, or there just isn't anything she likes. Picture the child who is withdrawn from friends, teachers, or other adults, who looks like she is trying to disappear. She may stare blankly, daydream, look through you, not hear what you are saying, or forget what you just told her. This is the child who is underaroused or dissociated. Dissociation occurs when we disengage from life outside of us and attend to an internal world.

One trauma survivor described the dichotomy of underarousal in this way: "You feel like a duck. You're sitting on the water all regal but you're pedaling like hell underneath." Another trauma survivor said that with underarousal, "It's like your body stops, but your insides keep moving." The underaroused pattern only *looks* like the trauma survivor is calm and less aroused than in the case of the overaroused pattern. Inside, however, the nervous system is just as revved.

Some traumatized children may demonstrate one or the other response pattern most of the time, but others may display both of them at different times throughout the same day. Some children alternate between shutting down completely when something challenges them, and jumping out of their seat to look for a fight for no apparent reason. They may alternate between staring blankly for several minutes at a time, daydreaming, and then accusing their siblings or classmates of looking at them funny and threatening or provoking them.

Additional signs and symptoms of extreme stress or traumatization are as follows:

- fears, anxieties, worries, nervousness, thoughts of doom (i.e. fear of dying/having shortened life)
- psychosomatic complaints (i.e. sore tummy, headache, sore limbs, aches and pains)
- inattentiveness, distractibility, difficulty concentrating, confusion, in a daze
- spacey, "floating through life," daydreaming, out of body experiences
- tantrum behaviors, easily upset, difficult to soothe, excessive crying
- anger, rage, aggression, violence, threatens and/or attacks others
- self-injurious behaviors (i.e. cutting, mutilating, threatens or attempts suicide)

- difficulty processing, learning, and retaining information; difficulty retrieving information already learned
- compulsive behaviors (i.e. excessive talking, getting up and sitting down, hitting others)
- eating disturbances (i.e. eating too much or too little)
- sleep disturbances (i.e. sleeping too much or too little, nightmares, sleepwalking, night terrors)
- attention-seeking behaviors
- anxiety disorders (i.e. school phobia, separation anxiety disorder, obsessive-compulsive disorder, panic attacks)
- ADHD-looking behaviors (i.e. can't sit still, can't concentrate, "ants in the pants")
- reenactment of the trauma (i.e. obsessive thoughts regarding guns, death, looks for fights and/or dangerous situations, fearless, instigates punishments)
- difficult to engage, avoids or refuses to work
- perfectionist, rigid, inflexible (i.e. big upsets over small mistakes)
- enuresis (wets pants), encopresis (soils pants)
- self-medicates (i.e. sniffs glue, smokes marijuana)
- bullies or is the "scapegoat"
- excessive clinging
- easily startled and jumpy
- irritable and agitated
- withdrawn from family and friends
- sad, listless, lethargic, sluggish
- extreme sensitivity to light and sound
- sexual acting out
- fear of going crazy

While children who are not chronically stressed or traumatized may exhibit one or more of these signs and symptoms some of the time, it is when children show such difficulties over a prolonged period of time that we must be willing to investigate the cause, especially if their academic or social functioning is suffering.

5
How Do Children Become Traumatized?

When our children perceive and thereby experience threat or terror, their brain automatically sends a message to the rest of the body to prepare for survival, a response otherwise known as "fight or flight." If they are able to complete their instinctive impulses to fight or flee, then the stress hormones and biochemicals released by the brain for survival are used up and are not left in the body to wreak havoc later.

It is when there exists no possibility of successfully fighting or fleeing - when powerful energy becomes mobilized for movement and movement is not an option - that trauma rears its ugly head. Biologically, the body makes the only other choice available at such a time. The instinctive choice to freeze is made when that is the best way to ensure survival. As is often the case with our children, they become immobilized by extreme stress or trauma not only when the body instinctively goes into freeze, but also when, because of physical limitations, they simply cannot override what is happening to them. Being restrained for a medical or dental procedure is an example of when this can happen.

Children are often rendered helpless. Their attempts to fight or flee are thwarted by the physical impossibility of the task. It is in this helplessness response, this immobility or freeze, where the seeds of traumatization are planted. Without being able to move, expend, and thereby discharge all of the chemicals and energies mobilized to meet the threat, our children are left with these powerful energies and chemicals trapped inside their body.

When the autonomic nervous system becomes deregulated in this way, any or all of the basic human drive functions can begin to operate irregularly, effectively out of balance. Body temperature may become irregular, such as in the case of shock when the body becomes cold. Children who are extremely stressed or traumatized may then experience a cooler body temperature than before. They may begin experiencing sleep disturbances and/or eating disturbances – gaining or losing weight, having difficulty falling asleep or staying asleep. These are functions mediated by the autonomic nervous system, the same system that is highly aroused when preparing for survival.

There are two branches of the autonomic nervous system: sympathetic and parasympathetic. Sympathetic nervous system responses are those that have to do with the body revving up for action, such as blood pressure accelerating, heart rate accelerating, face flushing, sweating, and muscles constricting. Parasympathetic nervous system responses are those that deescalate or relax the responses of the sympathetic branch. More relaxed and untraumatized children have a balance between these two branches. They are able to navigate through life's challenges with the ease of an ebb and flow. They may become upset by daily events but are able to self-soothe or receive the help of others without becoming stuck on high, or stuck on low.

Chronically stressed or traumatized children, on the other hand, have a nervous system that is out of balance. It does not ebb and flow with ease. It is either too revved up too much of the time, easily upset and difficult to soothe, or is too shut down lacking in vitality and participation in life. It is important for us, as parents, to recognize whether our children have a balanced nervous system that is flexible and adaptable to the normal stresses of life or not. If not, when we see the signs that they are out of balance, we must take the steps necessary to help foster in our children this important ebb and flow. (Chapter 10 lists many of these steps.)

6
How Could I Have Not Known?

Chronically stressed and traumatized children are misunderstood by most people not just parents. Parents, in fact, are the ones who often know something is wrong and ask for help but who get talked out of their concern by those around them, including professionals that often say the child will outgrow the problem or "will be just fine."

Chronically stressed and traumatized children are often misunderstood and labeled as being hyper, angry, inflexible, difficult, lazy, disabled, and moody. Michael, aged eight, was referred for "anger management" and "ADHD" symptoms yet had an extensive history of surgeries and medical procedures due to a lifelong kidney condition. Marisa, at five years of age, displayed "defiance" in her Kindergarten classroom two years after her ear was severed by a dog and then sewn back on. David, aged nine, was assessed for "emotional disturbance," yet as a two-year-old sustained serious injury to the head from a fall he had off a second story balcony. Oliver, as a six-year-old, was referred for "learning disabilities." He displayed memory problems, reading problems, and behavior problems after being hit by a car when he was riding his tricycle in an alley. Many of these children received clean bills of health from the physicians that served them at the time of their accident and thereafter, especially once their physical wounds were healed. It was parents, however, that knew everything was "not fine."

The fact that these children physically heal yet continue to display the residuals of their traumatic experiences becomes particularly evident in schools where poor academic performance and/or acting-out behaviors are observed. Chronically stressed and traumatized children are often considered for special education, in fact, because "something" is wrong, but what precisely too often remains a mystery. The dots are not connected between the events of children's lives and their difficulty functioning later.

Daniel

One quiet, mild-mannered, and intelligent fourteen-year-old boy, Daniel, was prone on occasion, to display violent rages that seemed uncharacteristic to him. Furthermore, they were terrifying to anyone who witnessed them. When I met with his parents and took a detailed developmental history, they did not remember the pregnancy and birth until my questions became more specific. In fact, they first responded that there was nothing remarkable to report about Daniel's delivery.

As I asked more detailed questions, however, and reflected their answers back to them by summarizing their statements, Daniel's parents began to realize how stressful the delivery really had been. They remembered that their son's heart rate was rapidly declining, as was the mother's, and that the medical staff cautioned they may quickly need to perform a C-section. Each parent remembered through the interview process that the experience had been "very stressful" to each of them. The C-section was not necessary in the end, but when Daniel was born, the umbilical cord was wrapped around his neck and he had difficulty breathing. He

You Can Heal Your Child

was placed in an incubator immediately after birth and kept there for two days until mother and child were released from the hospital.

I queried Daniel's parents further about whether or not he had experienced any other potentially traumatic experiences. Like most parents state when I ask them this question about their child, Daniel's parents reported that he had never experienced a trauma. However, when I asked about any serious accidents, falls, injuries, illnesses, hospitalizations, or medical procedures, it didn't take them long to recall the seemingly benign visit to the doctor's office when Daniel was two. A build-up of wax was removed from his ear, which may not have been a significant event for another person, but Daniel's survival instincts were mobilized as he was told to lay back and was restrained while the doctor dug for the wax.

Many years later, Daniel still had extreme reactions when anyone came close to that side of his head or when he needed to visit a doctor, especially in the years immediately after the event. Furthermore, it was revealed that Daniel had been a victim of bullying on several occasions that greatly impacted his functioning at school. Together, these pieces of information told Daniel's story and helped us appreciate where his problematic behaviors were coming from and how we could help.

The first time I noticed that we began helping Daniel was at the meeting where we discussed the results of his evaluation. As the team reviewed the details of his story, Daniel listened with remarkable focus and ease. His body language and facial expressions clearly stated a sense of relaxation and relief that we finally understood why some of his behaviors were so extreme and beyond his control. He could trust that we would operate within the context of our understanding of him and head in the right direction in terms of intervention. His parents too were clearly relieved that together we arrived at a comprehensive understanding of what was going on with Daniel and how each of us could play a role in his recovery.

When we ask the right questions and piece together our children's *whole* story from the very beginning of their life, we too can get to the bottom of what is really going on and what we can do as parents, with the help of educators and others, to finally see the progress we are longing for.

7
Can Chronic Stress and Trauma
Change the Brain?

Yes. The fact that chronic stress and trauma change the brain, however, does not mean that with the right kinds of intervention we cannot do much to reverse the effects. This is very important to remember. With the right kind of help, children who have been traumatized can heal and regain much of their pre-trauma abilities.

Let us consider how chronic stress and trauma change the brain in order to understand what we can do to help:

Once chronically stressed or traumatized, children's baseline levels of arousal and anxiety become elevated or "stuck on high," even when they *look* like they are underaroused. This is the result of several different neural and biochemical systems responding to the experience(s) of prolonged stress or terror. For instance, people who have been traumatized develop abnormalities in the release of brain chemicals that regulate arousal and attention (van der Kolk, 2002). In *un*traumatized children, stress activates all the principle anti-stress hormones which enable active coping behaviors. In traumatized children, however, relatively low levels of these anti-stress hormones exist causing an inability to regulate or manage responses to stress (van der Kolk, 2002). What this means for our children is that they can become easily overwhelmed by the demands of their environment, at home, in school, and otherwise.

The elevated baseline levels of arousal and anxiety in chronically stressed and traumatized children leave them in a persistent and biologically-based state of low-level fear (Perry, Pollard, Blakley, Baker, & Vigilante, 1995). Their more sensitive system can now become highly aroused by what we may consider minor stressors, such as the behavioral and academic demands of attending school.

Research in the field of psychology has for decades made us aware of the need for an optimal level of arousal in order for learning and prosocial behavior to take place. Arousal has the potential to stimulate learning, memory, and performance when it is optimal, and has the potential to inhibit learning, memory, and performance when it is in excess of what can be comfortably regulated by the learner's nervous system. When functioning within the optimal zone of arousal, children are able to process, integrate, and remember information, as well as behave adaptively. This is central to our understanding of children who have great difficulty learning, performing in the classroom, or meeting the social demands of their world.

High levels of arousal interfere with information processing and performance in all people, not just children. Advocates in the field of health and medicine today recommend that patients bring a friend or family member with them to the doctor's office when facing potentially life-threatening conditions. This is because we know how difficult it is for patients to process information while in a highly aroused state. Any one of us who has had to face this alone knows how little we remembered of what the doctor said. Only after getting into the safety of our own home, for instance, do we think of all the questions we had wanted to ask but forgot in the moment.

The chronically stressed or traumatized child has particular difficulty processing *verbal* information. Various studies assessing trauma's impact on the brain, for example, found increased activity in the right hemisphere and decreased activity in the left hemisphere (Teicher, 2000; van der Kolk, 2002). The right hemisphere is involved in nonverbal processing and the left hemisphere is responsible for language processing.

High levels of arousal cause our children to feel more anxious, and when more anxious, closer attention is paid to nonverbal than verbal cues (Perry et al., 1995). Chronically stressed and traumatized children actually become fixated on nonverbal cues that may aid in their survival, even when no real threat in the present moment exists. Remember, they live in a state of low-level fear most of the time, driven constantly to be ready for the next threat, whether real or perceived. Their brain's first and only concern when feeling threatened is survival, not getting along with others or reading, writing, and arithmetic. Behavioral and academic demands are ignored when the focus of the brain is survival.

By extension of their difficulty processing verbal information, chronically stressed and traumatized children also have great difficulty following directions, recalling what was heard, and making sense out of what was just said (Steele & Raider, 2001). Focusing, attending, retaining and recalling verbal information are all difficult tasks for the traumatized child, as is problem-solving (Yang & Clum, 2000).

Finally, the chronic high state of arousal that traumatized children live in interferes with learning by interfering with the functioning of the hippocampus, the part of the brain responsible for memory. One study found that traumatized children have lower memory volume in their left-brain hippocampal areas (Bremmer, Krystal, Charnez, & Southwick, 1996) while another study found that the stress involved in trauma caused the release of hormones that damaged the left hippocampal area thereby increasing memory deficit. REM sleep, a critical agent in the consolidation of memory, is disturbed in those with unresolved trauma (Siegel, 2003).

It is nearly impossible for our children to consolidate memories – working memory into short-term memory and short-term memory into long-term memory – when they cannot concentrate. Children are less capable of concentrating when they are in a chronic state of high arousal or anxiety. Both short-term (Starknum, Gebarski, Berent, & Schterngart, 1992) and verbal or explicit memory (Bremmer et al., 1996) suffer when people are in this state.

Whether it is learning in school that is negatively impacted or behaving adaptively in any other setting, the hormonal and biochemical changes that are a result of chronic stress and trauma inhibit children's abilities to cope, manage, and tolerate the often increasing demands of daily life.

8
What Can We Do to Prevent Problems for Our Children?

In order to prevent the unwanted alterations to the brain related to many of the learning and behavior problems our children experience, we must be willing to parent our children in very specific ways from the earliest moments of their life. The brain does not stop developing at birth. In fact, healthy brain development is largely dependent on experience, that is, interactions with people in the environment. While massive brain development occurs when our children are in the womb, another large amount occurs in the first four years of life.

Our children, like the rest of us, are born with only the brain stem fully developed. The first years of life involve rapid growth of both the limbic system and the neocortex. The limbic system is the emotional part of the brain and the neocortex is the more cognitive, rational part. Additionally, millions of neural connections between brain systems are formed in the weeks, months, and years after birth. The parts of the brain that are stimulated or activated at the time their neural connections are developing naturally become more charged (Perry, 2003).

Maternal heart rate is a major organizer in the development of the brain stem, which plays a major role in self-regulation capabilities. Self-regulation is now understood as the single most important foundational capacity for the possibility of higher-order learning and adaptive behavior. (See chapter 13 for more.) When a pregnant mother is able to manage everyday stress levels with self-soothing and self-care, the unborn child's brain stem develops normally.

However, when a pregnant mother experiences an inordinate amount of stress that is too great or prolonged to be moderated in a healthy way, the unborn infant's brain stem and its self-regulatory capabilities develop irregularly. Neural disorganization in the infant becomes possible. When the brain is changed in this way, regulation is difficult. External chaos leads to internal chaos or chaotic neural development, making the physiology of the pregnant mother critical to the unborn child (Perry, 2003). [It is important to state that stress should not be avoided by a pregnant mother (or anyone else). According to Dr. Perry, well-regulated stress response patterns are important to the development of self-regulation. The degree to which stress is experienced *with sufficient modulation* is what matters.]

Furthermore, at birth, the sympathetic branch of the autonomic nervous system is all that is available to the regulation of the infant. Thus, the infant is ready for responses of excitation and arousal, but without the parasympathetic branch (as it is still undeveloped) the infant has no way of calming or decreasing sympathetic responses.

The two branches of the parasympathetic nervous system include the dorsal vagal and the ventral vagal. It is the ventral vagal branch specifically that gets larger as children develop. This is the branch that modulates arousal and helps us feel calm again. This is extremely important. Newly born infants, until that ventral vagal branch of the parasympathetic nervous system is fully developed, are completely dependent on their caregivers for regulation of their experiences, sensations and emotions. This has profound implications when we consider the importance of our role as parents in preventing problems for our developing children. Our responsiveness to their needs in a timely fashion with great care and affection is essential to the healthy development of what we now know is necessary for learning and adaptive behavior – *self-regulation* of internal states of arousal.

When extreme stress or trauma is experienced in the earliest years of life, during gestation (in the womb) or the first years after birth, the unborn or newly born infant has no way of modulating their sympathetic nervous system's responses. Their heart rate, blood pressure, motor constriction, hormone and neurotransmitter levels all escalate during stress or trauma and then have no way *on their own* of returning back to baseline. The nervous system stays on high exhausting all efforts and resources. The infant is a "subcortical creature who lacks the means for modulation of behavior" that will only come with later development (van der Kolk, 2002).

As our infants and toddlers grow, their ability to regulate their own physiology in a balanced manner develops a more autonomous capacity over time. Until then, they are completely dependent upon the quality of our responsiveness. Perry (2003) and Schore (1994) among others argue that, in conjunction with genetic endowment, the nature of interactions between caregivers and their infants literally organizes the infant's brain. The more a particular parenting pattern is used, healthy or not, the more it fires that same pattern of neural activation becoming more deeply entrenched in the brain.

Parenting

The importance of at least "good-enough" parenting cannot be overstated when we consider the infant's dependence on caregivers to modulate their arousal. When pregnant or new mothers actively modulate their own stress levels, they directly and indirectly, modulate the stress levels of their babies. When this does not happen often enough, the baby's nervous system remains revved by the stress it experiences as a result of the anxiety the mother experiences. Stress hormones, released throughout the body during times of stress, remain in the babies' tiny body impacting their rapidly developing brain until they are sufficiently soothed. If soothing does not happen, or does not happen enough, babies are left in a state of high arousal until so exhausted they collapse into a complete shut-down.

It is the primary caregiver-infant relationship that regulates the infant's psychobiological states, thereby allowing the child to tolerate more intense and longer lasting levels of heightened, yet modulated, arousal (Schore, 1998). When we actively help our infant move from negative states of discomfort, hunger, and frustration, for example, to more positive ones, their emotions are successfully regulated and balanced. When our infants are not helped by us in a timely fashion to move out of negative states, they are left without any means of balancing out their own system, setting them up biologically for little tolerance of stress in the future.

When we are unable to co-create an attachment bond with our infant that allows for the dyadic regulation of emotion (because of post-partum depression, for example), the result is a biological state of shame in our baby (Stroufe, 1996). Shame is a painful infant distress state that is the result of the misattunement of infant and caregiver. Misattunement occurs when the infant comes to expect a positive response from the mother, such as a loving gaze, and receives instead a look of despair, for example. When this happens unexpectedly for infants, they are propelled further into the negative state they were already experiencing, one they cannot yet autoregulate or modulate on their own.

Shame itself does not cause the lack of self-regulation we may later see in our children. Shame can be successfully regulated through a process of "disruption and repair." If we are able to monitor and regulate our own affect and reengage with our infant regularly, then shame does not necessarily lead to problems for our child later. It is when we do not monitor and regulate our own affect, and when we are unable or unwilling to repair, that an enduring disposition to shame is possible (Schore, 1998).

Poor attachment and multiple experiences of misattunement between caregiver and child can be traumatic experiences for infants who are left in an aroused and negative state to fend for themselves without the resources to do so effectively on their own. Extremely stressful or traumatic events themselves, separate from parenting issues, have the same effect.

Attachment

A secure attachment is the result of contingent communication between caregiver and infant; it occurs when we are able to share and amplify positive emotions as well as share and soothe negative ones (Siegel, 2003). This is the kind of attachment that helps prevent the development of learning, emotional, and behavioral problems in our children. Insecure attachments are the result of inconsistent responding and availability of caregivers for sensitive, contingent communications with the infant.

Dr. Siegel and his research colleagues have found that unresolved trauma and grief in a parent can produce insecure attachments that can then lead to disorganization in the child (Siegel, 2003). When we have a compassionate understanding of ourselves we are able to provide the emotionally sensitive, contingent communication that our children need in order to thrive (Siegel, 2003). The question is not the presence of disruptions in the bonding or attachment between caregiver and infant. These disruptions are inevitable as none of us is perfect. What matters is the *balance* between disruption and repair. The more likely that mismatches between caregiver and infant are repaired, the more likely the infant will be securely attached. Again, *when we have a compassionate understanding of ourselves and our own stressful or traumatic experiences, repair is much more likely.* Considering the implications of trauma on later development throughout generations, we can see why it is so important that as a culture we find ways to understand chronic stress and trauma and effectively intervene as early as possible in order to resolve it in all generations.

When we resolve our own trauma and loss, we can be more responsive to our children. Better attunement of the parent to the child enables the child's brain to achieve bodily balance and later mental coherence (Siegel, 2003). Parent-child interactions shape the genetically programmed maturation of the brain to alter the ways in which emotion regulation and response to stress develop. In this way, secure attachment relationships promote well-being by supporting the integrative capacities of the child's developing brain (Siegel, 2003).

Before an Event

No matter how carefree we wish our children's lives could be challenges - such as a move to a new home or school, the need for a hospital visit or surgery, even a dental procedure - inevitably present themselves and require some form of stress management. Events such as these have the potential to be stressful or traumatic for our children but they certainly don't have to be. There is much we can do to ensure that changes, transitions, and other stressful events do not end up having terrifying effects on our children. With the right kind of approach to the event, the arousal that will likely be provoked can be modulated effectively.

One of the key characteristics of trauma is unpredictability, the feeling that without any notice, without the possibility for preparation, the ground is ripped from beneath our feet, shaking our core, and causing us to question if we have any control at all. There are important steps we can take as parents to prevent traumatization in our children, many of which have to do with increasing predictability through preparedness:

1. Gather all the facts about how the event will take place. In the case of a surgery, for example, be sure to inquire about the possibility of your presence throughout the procedure. Insist upon it as much as possible, and if you cannot attend, communicate your need to be there as much as possible, before and after.

2. If you notice that you are afraid, nervous, or anxious about the event, be sure to get your own support so you can stay strong and positive for your child. Being fully informed and having a plan for before, during, and after the event can be comforting, bringing your arousal levels down as well as your child's. Get all the support you need from family, friends, and others who help you to know you are not alone in helping your child.

3. Without distractions like television in the background, begin talking with your child about the upcoming event in a calm reassuring voice emphasizing that everything will be fine. In fact, suggest that the event could be an adventure during which your child will meet new people and have new experiences. (Just before bed is not a good time to have these discussions. It is preferable to talk about the event just after and/or just before an activity that brings your child comfort or joy.)

4. Remind children that they will not go through the event alone but will have your presence, love, and support at every possible point along the way. Let them know that it is your job to keep them safe and you will do everything in your power to do that.

5. Whenever possible, familiarize children with the specifics of the event. Take them to where the event will take place weeks, then days before. Walk them around the area pointing out anything you see that you know would be pleasing to them, again to familiarize them with the environment and to help them feel less threatened by it. Depending on what the exact event will be, it would be helpful to have your child meet the new neighbor, new

teacher, or the nurse, doctor, or dentist that will be present during the event.

6. Let children know they can ask as many questions about the event as they would like. In a quiet and calm setting, answer their questions as best you can always emphasizing that you will be with them at all times. If you don't have the answer to any of their questions, call someone who does and let your child know you will get back to him or her.

7. Remind children of their strengths, all the qualities they possess that have helped them get through other challenges in life. If they are compassionate and love to be a helper, find out how they could be an aide to other children if they are to be in the hospital, or how they would go about helping younger children in need of assistance if they are moving to a new school.

8. Be sure children are engaging in their resources, spending time doing the things they love, seeing the people that help them feel safe and cared for, spending time in places that bring them a sense of calm, comfort, and joy. Remind them of all the people who love and take care of them that will be there to support them through the event. One of the most important resources for them at this time is their sense of competence - that they are good at something. Provide numerous opportunities for them to master what they do well.

9. Keep routines, rituals, rules, and compassionate consequences for unacceptable behaviors in place. This is not the time to make

additional changes to what they expect, even if you think you should be easier on them. At this time especially, children need to know that their lives will remain as much the same as possible and there are still things they can count on. If you feel you need to be "easier" on them, offer more physical support and affection, more verbal reassurance of your love and support than you normally would, but keep boundaries and limits in place.

10. Whenever possible before, during, and after the event, ground children and help them notice their physical sensations until those sensations change from less to more pleasant. (Read chapter 10 for more.)

We began the chapter asking the question, "What Can We Do to Prevent Problems in Our Children?" In answering this question, I hope we have learned that if we want to prevent the development of problems in our children we have to start with our own healing first. When we are healed, or at least working towards the healing of our own grief and/or trauma with awareness and compassion for where we are on that path, we are more available to meet the needs of our children in a healthy way.

9
Can the Effects of Chronic Stress and Trauma be Healed?

Yes! Yet so many people continue to suffer for years, even decades - regardless of various forms of therapy. This is because most forms of therapy involve the so-called "talking cure" which engages the part of the brain least involved in the experience of stress and trauma.

Remember, when we are chronically stressed or impacted by a traumatic event, we become overwhelmed – not just psychologically, in our mind, but physiologically as well, in our body. During overwhelm, we become governed by the oldest part of our brain, the brain stem, the part of us that mediates our sensations and processes all of our sensory experiences. The brain stem overrides our newer, more rational, cognitive brain, the part of us that mediates higher order processing of language, especially words. It is the brain stem with its focus on nonverbal cues for survival that needs to be more engaged in the therapeutic process in order for therapy to work in the long-term.

Through the language of sensations – not thoughts or feelings, but *sensations* - it becomes possible to engage our old brain or brain stem. When we incorporate the body and its physical sensations into therapy, trauma can be healed. The pervasive view as a result of the commonly used medical model is that symptoms of post-traumatic stress constitute a lifelong disorder that can only be managed with medication and therapy. This is not the case. I have seen firsthand how these natural yet persistent responses to chronic stress or trauma can be healed completely when the body and its sensations are integrated into treatment.

To more fully understand how to heal the effects of chronic stress and trauma, we must turn to an unexpected place – the wild. As strange as this may sound, we have a great deal to learn from animals in the wild. Wild animals actually face stress and trauma daily and yet do not become traumatized. This realization regarding animals' lack of trauma response is important with respect to humans because we share a large portion of our brain with animals. Even though we may not know it, we have the same natural and innate capacity to move through trauma as animals do. What we must do in order to use this innate capacity to its greatest potential, as efficiently as animals do, is get out of our own way. We must let our brain stem do what it does best without interference from our newer more rational, cognitive brain, unique to us as humans.

The key to healing traumatic symptoms in humans lies in our ability to mirror the fluid adaptation of wild animals as they shake out and pass through the freeze or immobility response and become fully mobile and functional again (Levine, 1997). We have all heard the saying, "playing possum." We know that in nature there is a natural and active process involving predator and prey. When a prey, such as an impala, is aware of an impending predator, such as a cheetah, it has three biological choices, just as humans do. The impala can fight the cheetah, which will most likely not secure its survival, or the impala can flee from the cheetah, which is often what happens. However, if the impala begins to flee and goes as fast as it can and cannot outrun the cheetah, the impala will "play possum." It will exercise its third biological option – freeze – in order to survive.

What is important to remember is that all the energy that was mobilized for the impala to run fast and escape the cheetah is still in the "frozen" impala's body. The impala is as revved up as ever. It is simply not moving. This will sometimes save the impala's life because of the cheetah's enjoyment of the chase, the fight, and overall challenge of catching an active prey. The freeze sometimes makes the impala less interesting to the cheetah and it will leave it alone.

This is not the end of the story, however. What is most important to the understanding of how to heal trauma is what happens to the impala after the cheetah has abandoned it. After the impala has determined that it is safe to come out of the freeze, it will remain in its place while gently shaking and trembling until the shaking and trembling come to a natural end. Through the shaking and trembling, the impala's nervous system discharges all the residual energy that was mobilized for fight or flight but was left unused because of the impala's inability to fight or flee. The freeze or immobility response occurred not because the energy was gone. The energy was just as great even though the body was motionless. The freeze occurred because the brain recognized that it was that particular biological choice that would give the organism its best chance of survival.

The critical thing that animals in the wild do after a traumatic event that humans do not do, is allow time and space for the discharge of the mobilized energy to shake itself out of the nervous system. Instead, we quickly start thinking, fearing, talking, or moving.

One time, as I stood waiting at a traffic light, an elderly man fell off his bicycle in front of me. He was clearly shaken. I encouraged him to come over to the side away from traffic and just sit and let me comfort him as he rested. "Oh no! I'm fine!" he shouted as he climbed back up on his bicycle, shaking visibly. He was unsteady on his bicycle, thrown off kilter by the fall. I let him know how helpful it would be for him to just sit and let his body recover from the fall. I stressed that it would only take a couple of minutes, but he would not hear it. Perhaps it is the shame of the fall, the embarrassment that makes us want to act like it did not happen and carry on.

The man's fall was a relatively minor event. However, we often respond in this same way regardless of how major the event is. We convince ourselves that the quicker we get up on our two feet and resume duty, as if the event never happened, the better off we will be. Our newer, cognitive, more rational brain interferes with the reptilian brain's ability to shake off the event through gentle trembling and shaking that does not take longer than a few minutes in many cases.

The good news is that even if the man begins to develop posttraumatic stress responses from the fall, such as a fear of getting back up on a bicycle, or incessant shakiness and unsteadiness while on a bike, he can heal from the event and no longer experience such responses. The residual energy that was left in his body after the fall that he did not allow the time to shake off immediately after the event can still be discharged at a later time (as illustrated in chapters 12 & 13).

10
How Can I Help My Child?

The following list details the many things we can do either to help prevent problems from ever developing in the first place, or to intervene with a problem that has developed by soothing our child's overly aroused nervous system back into balance:

1. First recognize that your own internal state completely affects your child's internal state. Children absorb the energy - calm or anxious - of their parents and other adults like a sponge absorbs water. Recognize that your own chronic stress or unresolved trauma may get triggered by your child's experience and cause you to have an anxious internal state that will interfere with your child's ability to calm and heal. Seek the support of family and friends, or a professional, if need be for your own healing of unresolved trauma. Attending to your personal well-being allows you to be balanced and well-resourced for your child. Some of the most important ways to create balance in your life include getting your sleep, eating healthy foods, exercising, spending time in nature, and taking things *off* your to-do list.

2. Surround your child with affectionate loved ones who will act as a healing community for him or her. Do not allow your child to isolate. Healing takes place in communion with other people who remind us that we are not alone and that together we can get through anything.

3. Help orient your child to the world around him or her. Extremely stressed or traumatized people tend to go into dark, internal places that only reinforce their suffering. Being outdoors in nature is a powerful resource for healing. In nature, we can help orient our children to the trees, the breeze brushing through the leaves, the sun warming the skin. Whether outside or inside, have children look around and notice the resources that are there – pleasant sights, sounds, smells, and tactile experiences, such as the soft cushion of the couch beneath them or the coolness of the grass when they touch the earth.

4. Play a simple game called, "I See, I Hear, I Sense," during which you take turns naming something you see, something you hear, and something you sense inside your body. Take turns reporting a physical sensation you notice in your body, such as warm, cold, jumpy, calm, tight, tense, relaxed, butterflies, tingles, strong, weak, solid, soft, et cetera. After your child reports a sensation, encourage him or her to focus on the sensation until it changes. It always does without having to make it happen. If an unpleasant sensation lasts more than a minute or two without shifting, simply have your child feel the ground beneath him or her and orient to the world around and the sensation will change.

5. In trauma, people lose their ground - their sense of connectedness to themselves, to the earth, to nature, and to other people. Help children re-establish a sense of ground by having them sit in a chair with their feet firmly planted on the floor. Have children notice how they are being supported by the chair and the floor. Have them locate their center of gravity in the abdomen area by

having them place their hands on their belly and focus on their breathing. Encourage children to fill their belly with air as they take a deep breath in through the nose.

Stress and trauma often restrict breathing patterns to the chest area, keeping oxygen from the rest of the body. Having your child experience a fuller, deeper breath that nourishes a larger region of the body is a helpful intervention. Breathing in through the nose engages the part of the nervous system that helps calm and relax, whereas breathing in through the mouth engages the part of the nervous system responsible for accelerated heart rate and blood pressure. You can redirect children's breathing very simply so they experience a greater sense of ease.

6. Maintain a moderately quiet, safe place at home within which your child can live and work as peacefully as possible. Loud music or noises, especially yelling, can keep the arousal level of a stressed or traumatized child very high. Keep television news, violent video games, and other disturbing stories and images away from your child's attention.

7. The high arousal levels of stressed and traumatized children require firm yet flexible limits and boundaries that provide predictability. Although they will test these boundaries with various challenging behaviors, what they really crave is the containment that limits provide. Consistently apply the same consequence for the same behavior. The more that stressed or traumatized children can predict exactly what will happen if they behave a certain way, the safer they will come to feel in their environment. Daily

and/or weekly routines and rituals are effective ways to bring pre-dictability to a child's life.

8. You cannot positively acknowledge your stressed or traumatized child too much. In order to develop a much-needed sense of competency, value, worth, pride, satisfaction, and strength, children need to receive positive recognition. Consistently reward your child for desirable behaviors, with a smile, a hug, and an encouraging word.

9. Use time-out effectively by first teaching yourself and then your child to connect with bodily sensations in order to use them as signals. Bodily sensations of heat, rapid heart rate, tightness, or tension, for example, may signal the need for time away from others in a safe, non-punitive place. Having such a place to go to as a resource – without being banished there punitively – can help the nervous system do what it needs to do to calm and return to balance (this can take up to twenty minutes).

10. Help your children build, maintain, and access resources, such as healthy friends, loving family members, and activities they are good at. When children participate in what they do well, they experience some of the most healing feelings of all – the important sense of "I can!" Trauma leads to both a psychological and physiological stance of "I can't. I have no control. I have no power." Feelings of competence and success can reverse the effects of trauma. Whether academic, athletic, artistic, or philanthropic (helpful to others), provide children with numerous opportunities to feel like they can do something with mastery. For instance,

have children teach you something they know, or help a younger child, tell a joke they think is funny, or be the center of attention, whatever helps them feel like they have a purpose and important contribution to make. Children need to know they matter and are here for a reason.

Some of the most important resources, those that soothe the nervous system within minutes include: *nature* – being outside, breathing in fresh air, touching the soft grass or moist soil, taking in all the sights, sounds, and smells of "the great outdoors"; *animals* – feeding the ducks, riding a horse, walking the dog, cuddling a kitten; *music* – listening to what is calming and/or inspiring, or making music with drums, voice, or any other instrument; *exercise* – especially walking, dancing, and stretching; *sleep* – the single best way to renew and restore the nervous system, sleep reduces stress hormones and increases the body's capacity to tolerate the next day's challenges; *good nutrition* – sugar, caffeine, and fast food can negatively affect the nervous system, whereas lean protein and fiber, as well as fresh fruits and vegetables help keep us within the optimal zone of arousal where learning and adaptive behavior are possible.

11. Offer your child "quiet connection" through gentle holding and very little talking. This can help facilitate the release or letting go of stress and anxiety. When holding your child, you may notice your child trembling, shaking, giving off heat or sweating, even yawning excessively. These responses are not only normal but also healthy and should not be interrupted but simply watched and

validated through brief statements like, "That's it. That's okay. Just let that happen. I am right here with you."

12. While it is unnecessary and sometimes harmful to have your child talk about a stressful or traumatizing event(s), if your child continually brings it up and wants to talk about it, it is important to emphasize at different points throughout the story what your child's resources were – who or what was helpful to him or her or the strengths he or she possessed that contributed to survival.

13. Educate your child's teachers and doctors about what your child is going through or has been through and what his or her particular needs are. Be cautious about accepting lifelong labels and prescriptions for medication. There are many alternative understandings and treatments that offer greater hope and have far fewer side effects. Please see the "Additional Resources" section of this book to consider all of your options.

11
What other Resources are Helpful to Children and Why?

A simple visual image may help us to appreciate the effect resources have on the nervous system of our children over time. Imagine the scales of justice. Now imagine all of what activates the sympathetic branch of the autonomic nervous system piled on to one side of the scales. These are the things that make life a challenge for our children - the increasing demands of school, the social expectations of a peer group, trying to please parents, coaches, teachers, and the added emotional strain of whatever personal challenge they may have, such as their parents' divorce, remarriage, or reconstituted family, or the death of a loved one. There are numerous possibilities. Children have as many stresses as the adults in their lives and they can become as worn down as we do. Sometimes, many times, we cannot change or fix anything about the reality of our child's life. Stress and trauma are a natural part of what it means to be alive.

What we *can* do is bring the scales into balance, not by trying to eliminate the challenges in life on the one side of the scale, but by piling resources on the other side to stimulate the calming effect of the parasympathetic branch of the autonomic nervous system. We have the power and ability to equip our children to handle, manage and tolerate both their internal and external challenges by helping them experience the good, the joy, and the pleasure that resources bring to the nervous system.

A resource is anything that is helpful to the child, anything that contributes to health, safety, comfort, balance, calm, and a sense of relief. Sometimes it is helpful to look to the past to help children remember how they once coped with a difficult situation or frightening event. This may help identify a missing resource in the present that needs to be restored.

Imaginary resources can be as powerful as real ones. Sometimes, when we know what children's imaginary resources are, we can help bring pieces of the imaginary into realization. Perhaps your child imagines a place of safety and comfort and there are elements of that visual image that can be created in his or her actual life. Imaginary resources often include hopes and dreams that can act as motivators or mobilizing forces for children.

One of the most powerful resources is your child's own body; more specifically, the balancing, soothing impact of his or her parasympathetic nervous system. When stressed and anxious, or when terrified from some previous traumatic event, our children no longer feel safe in their own body. They feel jumpy inside and afraid, as though something bad is about to happen. They feel as though the triggers that bring about these sensations and feelings are unpredictable and they have no control over them. This causes them to panic and draw inaccurate cognitive conclusions that the sensations and feelings are not going to go away on their own. In an effort to quickly avoid discomfort and pain, children will act-*out*, act-*in* (turn their frustration against themselves), or self-medicate, and we don't want that for them. We want them to know how to access healthy resources so they can resolve their pain and discomfort through the natural self-regulation of their internal states.

Regulation of the sympathetic and parasympathetic branches of the nervous system creates a physiological balance in the body between unpleasant and pleasurable sensations. As parents, we can give our children the opportunities they require to access resources that help them *experience* that balance externally and internally. This is precisely what makes life and all of its challenges more tolerable.

Sensory Awareness

Eugene Gendlin (1981), founder and author of *"Focusing,"* conducted important research to uncover the difference between people who get better from participating in therapy and those who do not. He found that the difference between the two groups was body or sensory awareness. The people that healed were those that noticed and experienced their bodily sensations and were able to share them with the therapist in the moment they became aware of them. They noticed when they were tight, tense, warm, cold, shaking, quivering, relaxed, or comfortable. They paid attention to where in their body they felt these and other sensations. They were able to notice the sensations, however uncomfortable, and focus on them until they shifted from less to more comfortable and tolerable. They had a palpable and total experience, involving both mind and body, of the physiological truth that "what goes up (sympathetic responses like tension), must come down (parasympathetic responses of relaxation)."

Many current authors recognize the importance of working with children at the level of sensation and provide descriptions of activities that help increase sensory awareness. For instance, in their book, *"Your Anxious Child,"* John S. Dacey and Lisa B. Fiore (2002) wrote that children are constantly bombarded by stimuli from the external environment and have thus lost track of their inner environment – their heart and breathing rates, pain in their joints, and tension in their muscles. Sensory awareness, according to the authors, is a way for children to discover what these inner experiences are and how they are affected by them. As children become aware of their inner worlds, they can be taught ways to alleviate stress and strain and, therefore, better deal with problems presented in the outside world. Looking again to our metaphor of the scales of justice, as we pile on resources such as sensory awareness to the one side of the scales, children are better able to tolerate and overcome the challenges piled on the other side.

Although the authors ascribe to a cognitive approach to working with anxious children (one that intervenes mostly with the mind and not the body), the first step of their COPE program is relevant to this discussion. "C" stands for calming the nervous system. The authors recognize the effects of stress on the nervous system, and the involvement of body sensations in the stress response. They describe sensory activities that help increase children's awareness of breathing, heart rate, and comfort levels. For instance, one important exercise described involves an exploration and experiencing of supportive surfaces. Children are encouraged to begin noticing what surfaces they find most comfortable – an armless chair, or an armed chair, a soft cushion, or the firm floor. The point that the authors make is an excellent introduction to exercises that involve children noticing how and when and under what conditions they are most comfort-

You Can Heal Your Child

able and supported. Paying attention to their inner environments – their bodily sensations - is required in order to arrive at an answer.

In her book *"Relax,"* author Catherine O'Neill (1993) helps children notice when they are feeling tense in their body by having them pay attention to the signals their body gives them, such as a "horrible feeling in [their] stomach." She teaches children in her well-illustrated book that when they are stressed they may sweat, blush or shake, clench their fists, bite their lips, or grind their teeth. The sympathetic nervous system is in full swing. Children learn about their body and its reactions in a way that is sensitive to the fact that there are times when they simply cannot think properly. The author wrote: "Your mind goes into a spin. You can't get the words out. You stammer. You can't understand what people are saying...[You] feel as though [you] are wound up like an elastic band, tighter and tighter, until [you] are ready to snap." Isn't it alarming to think that these are the very times we expect our children to count to ten and make a rational behavioral choice?

O'Neill included in her book a depiction of several different resources that help stimulate the parasympathetic nervous system – the opposite, more comfortable sensations than those just described. Just as with the image of the scales of justice, O'Neill wrote that sometimes we cannot make the things that make us tense go away. What we need to do is spend time doing things and being with people that balance out the tension. Resources that O'Neill described and depicted in her book include taking a bath, swinging on a hammock, cuddling up with a teddy bear, reading a book, and talking to someone trusted. These are not necessarily the things that will have a calming effect on all our children. Some of the above-mentioned activities may actually increase some children's anxiety depending on their personal history. The idea is to help identify and access the specific kinds of activities that *will* be soothing to them during times of need. The "secret key" to tolerance, healing, and self-regulation, according to O'Neill, is "keeping balance between tension and relaxation, sadness and happiness."

Visualization

Dr. Violet Oaklander's (1998) book, *"Windows to Our Children,"* is also full of sensory-related activities, including various visualizations that help children become more aware of their inner worlds. It is through these activities that children gain the experience of sensation and create body memories of what it is like to feel more relaxed and at peace. Visualization is especially valuable because of what research has revealed: When people visualize themselves engaged in an activity or being in a particular place, their brain fires neurons throughout their body as though they are actually having the experience. This can create *implicit memory* in the person – procedural or motor memory (also known as cellular or sense memory) of the visualized experience. When felt in the body and grounded in sensation even visualizations have lasting and transformative effects.

A now famous and well-known basketball study was done years ago to demonstrate the value of visualization (Wissel, 1994). Three groups of "basketball players" (subjects) were involved in the study. One group practiced their free-throws from the free-throw line on an actual basketball court. Another group was instructed not to practice at all. The third group of players was taught specific visualization techniques and told to use those rather than to actually physically practice. The third group was encouraged to see themselves at the free-throw line practicing their shots as though they were on the court doing it. The process of visualization involves more than sight. "It involves all the senses to create more vivid images" (Wissel, 1994). The research proved, in Wissel's words, that "the brain does not distinguish between imagined thoughts and real actions. When you mentally feel yourself shooting, it is as though you are actually shooting. [The] mental images will determine how well you actually do."

At the end of a specified practicing time frame, it was found that two of the three groups of players improved their free-throws substantially: The group that actually practiced *and* the group that only visualized the practicing. The players who only *saw* themselves practicing experienced their neurons firing throughout their body just as the players who actually practiced. This is because "the mind is like a computer. What you put into it is what comes out. Sensory input determines motor output" (Wissel, 1994). Both groups of players created new body memory stores. They each developed an implicit memory of taking the free-throw shots over and over, thereby improving their performance over time.

Visualization does not just improve athletic performance. A review of the research on the subject revealed the positive relationship between visualization and muscular relaxation, decreases in stress hormones, heart rate, galvanic skin response, breath frequency, and muscle tension (Gillis, 2003). Imagery of sprinting was found to increase tachypnea (an already increased rate of respiration) considerably, demonstrating that visualization can work effectively either way, to increase or decrease sympathetic nervous system responses.

Although visualization can be used to help children feel more relaxed, it is important to note that some children actually become highly activated when "relaxation" exercises are introduced. Having an agenda of relaxation can create tension and anxiety in children when they know there is an end goal in mind. It becomes something that must be achieved – an outcome they must attain. Our children have enough goals to meet. In my experience, they benefit more from our interventions when they know there is no agenda, no right or wrong answer, no evaluation of their "performance." By the same token, when children begin experiencing either pleasant or unpleasant sensations in their body, they need to be taught that pleasant sensations are not necessarily "good" while unpleasant sensations are "bad." They need to be encouraged *not* to try to change any sensation but simply to notice without judgment. Sensations just *are.* They do not have to be positive or pleasant to have value.

Roy Re-visited

After taking inventory of Roy's resources with both his father and stepmother, I asked Roy's father to bring him for joint sessions so I could meet with the two of them alone. Remember, Roy is the eleven-year-old boy whose mother suddenly died when he was seven (see chapter 3 for more).

In my first session with Roy and his father, I became more aware of what resources Roy had in his life to draw upon for strength and healing, and what needed to be restored or created anew. I asked his father to focus on three things in the weeks to come: 1) spending more time with Roy one-on-one, even if just fifteen more minutes a day; 2) having Roy (with or without the family) spend more time in nature and with his beloved pet dog; 3) creating a greater sense of safety for Roy with consistent rules and consequences for behavior, a daily and weekly schedule and routine, as well as verbal reassurance of his father's safety.

During our second session, Roy's father reported a decrease in the "drama" that was happening at bedtime. Roy was now procrastinating with homework. As we talked about the problem with his homework, I asked Roy to notice what was happening inside his body. He said he felt "jumpy" and "nervous." We did a visualization exercise that helped him imagine, and be in, his safe place, which he described in so much detail, I knew he must have been there before. I asked him to notice how he felt in his body as he thought of and described his safe place. He noticed how much calmer he was, that the nervous energy he had experienced earlier in the session was gone. I reminded Roy that he could go into his mind and be in that safe place anytime he needed to. Additionally, I had Roy tell me about the activities he loves doing, the places he loves being, and the people with whom he most enjoys spending time. I reminded his father to support and encourage Roy to engage in those resources as often as possible.

During our third session, I asked Roy to draw himself in the center of a page and write around his image the names of all the people who love and take care of him. Then I had him color the silhouette of a body with each color representing a different sensation or feeling. He was able to identify the feelings he senses in his body that he holds inside and does not express, and this led to an important conversation during which Roy's father admitted holding in his feelings of sadness too. He always felt he needed to be strong for his children after their mother's death. What he learned during this session was how it was more important now to openly express his grief, confusion, and sadness so that Roy could do the same.

In our fourth session, we continued with activities that reminded Roy of his strengths, gifts, talents and other resources. More importantly, he was guided to experience the effects of these resources in his body as he thought about and/or engaged in them. Once his nervous system benefitted from thinking about and experiencing his resources, we were able to talk calmly, without fear or agitation, about the things that worried Roy, the ways in which he felt different from his peers and others, and the secrets he felt he needed to keep from his family and the rest of the world. Approaching these topics after establishing safety and strength *in his body* meant they weren't so scary or overpowering anymore. I had Roy's father participate in the activities so Roy could witness his father being vulnerable, open, and honest as well.

For our fifth and final session, I gave Roy a piece of paper with the following written on top: "Some people think the spirit goes to heaven to be with God, and some think it takes a new form...like the caterpillar that becomes a butterfly. Others think the spirit becomes a part of those they loved. (Draw what you think.)" Roy smiled immediately after reading the sheet and quickly began drawing what he believed. He drew a big, beautiful butterfly that was purple and red and orange and green and blue, and he shared with me that his mother loved but-

terflies. He said he believed that every time a butterfly flies by or rests on a leaf close to him his mother is visiting and bringing him her love.

Before Roy left that day he asked me to please tell his story to help other children going through anything like what he experienced. I could see that Roy felt a powerful sense of relief that he wanted others to experience too.

12
What Kind of Therapy Works Best when a Child Needs More Help?

Brain- and body-based therapies that communicate with and soothe the nervous system, right hemisphere of the brain, and the brain stem help chronically stressed and traumatized children heal completely. Such a focus in therapy - on the brain and body - is necessary and effective because these are the parts of our children that are most involved in both their experiences of stress and trauma and their natural albeit challenging behaviors.

Jesus
(pronounced hay-soos)

I met nine-year-old Jesus at his new school at the request of the school counselor. He was sexually assaulted at his previous school on the playground by a group of peers. During recess at his new school, and any other time he was supposed to be on the playground, he would end up in the office crying. The counselor, who had already been meeting with Jesus to try and help him, introduced us and let Jesus know that it was he who had asked me to meet with him. Although Jesus was crying, he nodded that he would meet with me. When the counselor left, as Jesus continued to cry, I comforted him by placing my hand on his upper mid-back. I quietly waited simply letting him know that I was there to be with him and to help him. I assured him that everything was going to be okay. Jesus continued to cry. I decided to do some immediate grounding and invited him to sit with me on the floor.

We sat on the carpet and placed our hands on the ground at our sides. We sat a comfortable distance apart. I gave him a warm blanket that the counselor had in his office for use with students when they needed it. As he cried, I asked Jesus to feel the warm blanket resting on his lap and to get as comfortable as he could as he rubbed his hands over the carpet.

"Can you feel the ground beneath you, Jesus? Do you feel how strong and solid it is and how you are connected to it?"

"Yes," he told me as he continued to rub the floor. I encouraged him to take a moment and feel the parts of his body connected with the floor. I asked him to notice how his body was being supported by the floor, and to notice how his back was being supported by the wall he was leaning against. After a short time, he took a deep breath and his cry became more subdued.

I then told Jesus we were going to do an exercise that might seem a little funny. I told him he would need to squeeze his muscles, hold them a few seconds, and then let them go one at a time. I had him start with his toes and move all the way up his body. He squeezed, held, and released many of his muscle groups. By the time we were done, Jesus was remarkably calmer. I gave him words of encouragement letting him know what a great job he did with the exercise. We rested a moment.

It was time for a different activity. I asked Jesus to close his eyes if he could, letting him know that he could open his eyes when he needed to. I told him I was going to take him on a fantasy trip just by telling him a story, and asked him if that would be okay. Yes, he told me. Jesus closed his eyes and listened quietly as I led him through a visualization exercise. The specific visualization I chose was from Violet Oaklander's book, "Windows to Our Children." I modified it to help Jesus imagine a safe place. I guided him gently through the exercise and gave him plenty of time to enjoy being there in his imagination. I then asked him to draw the safe place he saw.

Jesus got up from the floor and sat at the table and saw the page I had left for him there. It was from one of Marge Heegaard's (1993) books for children. For the most part it was a blank sheet of paper at the top of which were the words, "It is _important_ to have a place that feels _very safe_. This can be a real place...or a pretend place to think about." Jesus read the page then drew a beautiful picture of a grassy meadow that had three red flowers in it and one large solid tree. Jesus drew the sun at the top of the page.

I encouraged Jesus to take a few moments to really look at his safe place and to imagine himself there. I let him know what a beautiful job he did and reminded him that if he ever needed to he could close his eyes and imagine himself in his safe place.

The last activity we did in this first session, which lasted approximately forty-five minutes, was another exercise at the table. I gave Jesus a sheet of paper that had the words, "I know how I like to be comforted," written on the top, also from Heegard's book. This sheet also read: "(draw this...

and then close your eyes and imagine it.)" At the bottom of the page it was written, "I can use words to let others know what I need."

On this sheet, Jesus drew two small pictures. One picture was of him shooting a basketball right into the hoop. The other was of him lying down on the floor playing a video game. The character he drew on the screen of the video game was a strong, muscular man flexing his arm muscles.

Although the counselor reported that he noticed a decrease in how upset Jesus would get when he was in the office, he still did not want to go out to the playground. We had more work to do. Together, Jesus and I went back to the floor for more grounding. It should be noted, that sitting on the ground is not necessary for the exercise. It can be done while standing or sitting on a chair. It is about feeling supported by and connected to the ground by calling attention to that connection.

Again, I had Jesus feel the ground beneath his hands, buttocks and legs. This time, I brought his attention to his breath. I taught him how to take deep breaths that would help center him when he was upset. I modeled a soothing breath – taking air in through the nose and out through the mouth - showing Jesus how to do it for himself. Keeping at least one hand on the belly, I explained the importance of taking a deep breath in through the nose and filling up the belly with air like a balloon. Remember, many people shaken by a crisis begin breathing less efficiently, with shorter breaths that permit air to reach down into the body only as far as the mid-torso area. Shallow breathing fills the lungs but not the belly. When we breathe deeply into the belly through the nose, we engage the parasympathetic nervous system for soothing and relaxation.

Jesus did as I did. He kept one hand on his belly, breathed deeply in through his nose and filled his belly up like a balloon. It took a couple of tries before he got the hang of it. Once our bellies were full, we slowly exhaled through the mouth. We repeated these deep breaths five times. Jesus was much calmer after just a few moments of this exercise.

I re-visited with Jesus the coloring worksheets he had done a week earlier. I did this to remind him of his safe place and how he likes to be comforted. I had him take a moment with his safe place to imagine himself there and then asked him what he noticed in his body. This prepared him for the next coloring exercise.

I gave Jesus a worksheet from my activities book, "Hope and Healing: An Activities Book for Any Adult Working with School-Aged Children (Melrose, 2006). It had a silhouette of a body on it and at the top of the page was the question, "Where are you feeling your feelings today?" There was a legend on the page that matched sensations with colors. I asked Jesus to color in the silhouette where he felt each of the sensations listed according to the legend. With the color blue, which signified "flowing," Jesus lightly colored in the silhouette from the waist down. With the color green, which signified "relaxed," Jesus lightly colored in the silhouette from the waist up. When he was finished, we talked about his picture and I asked him to notice if he could sense those sensations in his body in that moment. He confirmed that he was feeling relaxed in his upper body and flowing in his lower body. We rested for a moment taking time to allow for those sensations to be fully experienced.

There was one last worksheet to do. On the top of the page it said, "Some people believe they have a higher power, God, or guardian angel to watch over them. Do you?" Jesus took a moment and then drew and colored a picture of his sister in their home with an angel flying over her head. He also drew inside the home a shrine that had another angel flying over it. This is when Jesus began to weep. His cry was different this time. It was quiet and gentle and without hysteria. It was then that I put my hand on his back and said, "It's not your fault, Jesus. Those boys were wrong to do that to you. You did not deserve to have that happen. No one deserves that. It's not your fault." Jesus cried more deeply as he leaned into me with his arms wrapped around my back. I held him for several moments as I reassured him of what a good boy he was and how it was not his fault. He stopped crying and looked at me. I said, "You're going to be okay, Jesus. I know that. I'm meeting with your parents today and we're going to make sure we do everything we can so that you're okay."

At the end of the school day, Jesus' parents came to pick up Jesus. They came to the office with Jesus' sisters. Jesus was smiling proudly as he introduced me to his whole family. I met with his parents alone for approximately forty-five minutes. With the help of a translator, I explained to them what I thought was going on inside Jesus' body because of what had happened to him. I explained that when scary things happen they happen to the whole person, not just the mind, but the body as well. I let them know that Jesus was jumpy inside because he was still scared. He was worried for his sister, which they knew, because of how threatened and violated he was by those boys. He imagined that something terrible could also happen to his sister. He had become obsessed with taking care of her, to the point of running out of his classroom early everyday to pick her up at her classroom before the last bell rang.

I let Jesus' parents know that it was important for them to remain as calm around Jesus as possible. It would be important for them to take care of themselves with the help of their friends and family. That way they would be better equipped to take care of Jesus when he needed them. I asked them to begin to notice how they felt inside when Jesus got upset. If they noticed that they too were getting upset, I encouraged them to take deep breaths to calm themselves. I told them how children pick up how their parents are feeling and they become more upset as they can sense their parents becoming upset. It would be soothing to Jesus to be in the arms of his parents when they were calm and centered, breathing deeply and able to be a safe, comfortable place to fall. They said they could do that. They said they would give him plenty of physical affection as they made reassuring comments about how they would always be there for him and take care of him and his sisters. I let them know that Jesus may shake or tremble in their arms or at other times, or that he may get hot and sweaty. This was a good thing, I told them, and asked them not to stop it. I asked them to let Jesus know that that was his body's way of shaking everything off so he could feel better.

I asked Jesus' parents to turn off the television, especially the news, scary movies, and violent video games. The calmer they could keep the environment, the calmer Jesus would be. I explained that two of the most important things parents can do for children who have been traumatized are to provide as great a sense of safety as possible, and to create as many opportunities as possible for competency and mastery. I explained the importance of keeping Jesus involved in activities that would be both an outlet and a source of pride for him. Finally, I let Jesus' parents know that he needed to be reassured of their roles as his and his sisters' protectors.

I checked in with the counselor a week later to learn that Jesus had returned to playing out on the playground every recess and lunch. Months later, the counselor reported that Jesus had not been to the office crying since I had seen him last.

As you can see from my work with Jesus, this approach is different from most other forms of therapy. It is different because we have learned that with chronically stressed or traumatized children, internal states remain fundamentally unchanged after various kinds of interventions including traditional talk therapy. Traditional therapies and forms of counseling that attempt to change children's perceptions of the world and behaviors in the world, by means of reason and insight, using conditioning, behavior modification, and medication, simply do not work (Levine, 2003). World-renowned trauma expert, Dr. Bessel van der Kolk, stated at a national conference November 15, 2002, that therapists and their clients "may be having a nice time chatting" in a session of traditional therapy, "but they shouldn't be charging." Anyone who has been traumatized cannot be healed through the so-called "talking cure." Neuroscience is now showing that our emotional states originate in the conditions of our *body*. Both research and best practice indicate that we must look to new techniques that incorporate the body in a very specific way in order to see lasting change.

There are new therapies in the world of mental health that heal traumatized children remarkably. They are generally referred to as "somatic" because they involve the integration of the body and its sensations into therapy. Leading researchers in the field of stress, trauma, and the brain, Drs. Bruce Perry, Bessel van der Kolk, and Allan Schore, all indicate that the effects of stress and trauma can be healed through these more somatic approaches. Although different names are used for similar somatic therapies (i.e. Somatic Experiencing and Sensorimotor Psychotherapy), the approach I use with children with success is called Self-Regulation Therapy (SRT). I will review this approach in the following chapter.

13
What is Self-Regulation and Self-Regulation Therapy (SRT)?

Self-Regulation

The act of self-regulation involves the shifting from one bodily state to another. Children often get anxious or excited about an event or situation, for example, but soon enough come to experience a natural relaxation response that calms them and keeps their arousal levels within a tolerable range. Arousal levels involve both sensations and feelings. The ability to keep arousal within a tolerable range is critical to all tasks in life, whether educational, social, or interpersonal.

In order to attend, concentrate, assimilate and integrate new information, as well as perform tasks in a manner suitable to situational demands, the nervous system must be in an optimal state of arousal (Mercer & Snell, 1977). With healthy self-regulation, this optimal state is possible.

Self-Regulation Therapy (SRT)

SRT is a natural approach to healing the effects of chronic stress and trauma that works with the nervous system by engaging the body's sensations. SRT promotes the nervous system's capacity to reset itself back into balance and thereby restores the self-regulation of internal states. SRT has four essential elements: *building resources, completing "the incomplete behavior," integration,* and *psychoeducation and support.*

Building Resources

One of the most important resources that must be developed in the first stages of SRT is *safety*. The *relationship* between SRT providers and children is one of the most powerful ways to establish a sense of safety. Not only do providers need to be safe people in a safe environment during the SRT process, but they also need to work with children's parents and educators to help them provide a greater sense of safety for their children at home and in school.

One way both parents and SRT practitioners provide safety within the context of a caring relationship is to *understand* children, understand what is *really* going on. A second equally important step is to let children know they are understood. We need to communicate to them that we know they would control their behaviors better if they could and that we know they feel badly about it afterward. We need to reassure them that we understand they didn't mean to "mess up" again. Reminding children of their goodness and their healthy side, speaking to those parts, focusing on and amplifying those parts of our children goes a long way in establishing the kind of relationship that creates the level of safety needed to begin the process of healing.

There are disruptions to a sense of safety. These disruptions include asking too many questions, using too many words, requiring children to reason and come up with explanations for why they behaved as they did or behave as they do. Remember, chronically stressed and traumatized children have less access to the part of their brain that reasons and processes language. They have greater access to the part of their brain that is nonverbal and more sensory. What they need from us is physical support with a few select words that communicate that *we* understand. We need to voice that we don't need them to try and figure things out. As the adults in their life, *we* will figure things out. Furthermore, we need to tell them they are not alone.

Another disruption to their sense of safety is our inconsistency. Our inconsistency as parents means that we, like stress and trauma, are unpredictable. This reinforces for them what they have already come to believe from their devastating experiences - no one and nothing can be counted on. When we establish routines and rituals, on the other hand, and when we have explicit rules that have pre-determined consequences that we implement with consistency and compassion, we counter the unpredictable qualities of trauma and begin to undo their effects.

Some of the most important rules we can have as parents for our family in order to create safety for our children include no yelling, belittling, name-calling, making fun of one another, or laughing at each other. We often cannot control what our children must endure when they are away from us, but in our own home where we are responsible for their experience, there is much we can do to offset and thereby balance out what happens to them when they are with others.

In addition to establishing safety, providing children with opportunities to feel competent is something both parents and SRT practitioners can and must do. Tapping into, and expanding upon, a child's sense of competence is a necessary prerequisite condition for SRT to be effective. Many chronically stressed and traumatized children have a deeply imbedded state of shame rooted in both their psyche and their physiology. They feel hopeless, helpless, stupid, incapable, and/or out of control. It is our job to find what they can do well. We need to determine in what circumstances and with whom they *are* well, and highlight and encourage these things in a genuine and consistent way. When children feel both safe and competent within the context of a trusting relationship, the foundation for healing is laid.

In order to resolve the effects of trauma on the nervous system, we have to learn to communicate with the nervous system. The parts of the nervous system most involved in the experience of stress and trauma understand and respond to the language of sensations. Our children need to be taught sensation words and how these words describe their inner landscape. They need to be encouraged to notice *in the moment* what is happening inside their body as they have different experiences. This noticing in the present moment connects and integrates children with their more primitive brain where the secrets to resolving trauma reside. Within the implicit memory of the body unresolved trauma is "hidden," "waiting," and ready to be activated (Schore, 2003) in order to be resolved.

Once children begin to experience their bodily sensations in a more conscious way, they will come to notice that sometimes they have comfortable, pleasant sensations and other times they have uncomfortable, unpleasant sensations. Remember, by teaching children to focus their attention on their sensations without trying to change them they will come to notice that the sensations inevitably change on their own. They may change from pleasant to unpleasant or vice versa but they do not stay fixed, stuck, or the same. There is an ebb and flow as we discussed in chapter 5 that children will come to experience more readily through SRT. It is the noticing and experiencing of this ebb and flow that allows children to begin to understand that the body will take care of itself without our needing to interfere.

When unpleasant sensations seem to be taking over and do not seem to be changing quickly enough (always give it at least two minutes), introduce resources to children that help the physiology change. Mental representations of positive experiences, for example, have an impact on physiology causing the release of oxytocin, one of the body's natural opioids (Schore, 2003). Having children think of, and describe, their best friend or their safe place or a pet they love can help the nervous system regulate in those moments when it does not seem to be doing so on its own. This is how we teach our children to self-regulate, through *experiences* with their body that teach them their body can be trusted and it can mend.

Completing "The Incomplete Behavior"

As children begin to experience their body, they will notice sensations *and* they will notice *impulses* to do something. They may feel the impulse to run, kick, hit, or move their limbs in a particular direction, such as raise their hands in front of their face, fall to the floor, or roll to one side. The possibilities are endless. These are the body's implicit memories coming to life. The body remembers its responses to the trauma because they were left incomplete.

Children who undergo medical procedures, for example, are often so afraid of what is happening to them their body attempts to engage in defensive responses, such as running away from the hospital or fighting off the doctors. These impulses to defend are thwarted, however, when they are restrained or placed under anesthesia. Under such conditions, children are unable to complete the impulses of their body to run or fight. The defensive energy and corresponding impulses are left in the body waiting for completion. When the energy and impulses are re-triggered, the body re-enacts the trauma hoping to complete the response. Completion cannot happen in this way, however. *Re-enactment* of the trauma is disconnected, dissociated, and harmful.

The re-enactment traumatized children experience only serves to more deeply entrench the maladaptive circuitry in their brain perpetuating the deregulation of their nervous system and problematic behaviors. The body's resources must be accessed through the language of sensations. Once the language of sensations is spoken, the incomplete behavior or unresolved trauma that is waiting to resolve can be completed. With the SRT provider's gentle support and quiet encouragement, children may be helped to complete the response.

Completion of the thwarted behavior must happen slowly within the context of a safe relationship. It is critical that despite children wanting to act on the impulse quickly and with vigor, they are slowed down and encouraged simply to *imagine* themselves completing the behavior, seeing it in their mind's eye while noticing the sensations in their body and how they change. A physiological discharge may occur when children imagine the completion of the response. They may become warm or hot, turn red or begin to perspire. They may tremble or shake. They may yawn widely and repeatedly. They may laugh or cry. These are all signs of discharge indicating the completion of something powerful that was left undone.

One child I worked with to complete an incomplete behavior had been diagnosed with both ADHD and OCD (Obsessive-Compulsive Disorder), rather than with post-traumatic stress, which I felt was the more appropriate way to conceptualize his anxiety and "hyperactivity" (really hypervigilance). He was sexually violated at the age of four by his stepmother. He was seven when I worked with him.

Cooper

I saw Cooper once a week for a period of eight weeks. In our fourth session together, we continued the process of building the resources of relationship, competency, and safety. A visualization activity was utilized to help Cooper establish a safe place. Once the exercise was complete and he was asked to draw the safe place he saw, he instead drew scribbles all over the page with a black crayon. When I asked him what he drew he said it was "her," his step-mother, and when I asked him about it further, he said he saw her all the time.

I asked Cooper to notice what he was feeling inside his body as he looked at the picture of black scribbles and he said he wanted to run. I encouraged him to allow that impulse to surface and notice where in his body it was. He said his legs. "That's right," I said, "Feel your legs wanting to run. Now without actually running, I want you to picture the place you want to run to. Can you see it?" "Yes," he said, "It's a tree. I want to run to that tree." "That's it, Cooper," I said. "Now I want you to see yourself running to that tree. Run and don't stop until you are safe in that tree." Cooper's face became very flush and I could feel the heat emanating from his body. Once he was up in the tree, I encouraged him to rest there, to take his time, and notice how he felt inside now that he was in the tree and safe. Within minutes, Cooper became more settled and relaxed.

At that point, I let Cooper know he could do to the picture he drew whatever he wanted. Without hesitation, he scrunched it up into a tight little ball, stomped on it, threw it into the trashcan, and shut the trashcan outside the door of my office.

The next time I saw Cooper, two weeks later, was the first time I had seen him in over two months without a large red circle of dry, flaky skin around his lips from compulsively licking them. He looked more vibrant and alive. In fact, I had never before seen him look so completely healthy. I was struck by the difference in him and I sensed he had made tremendous progress.

Sadly, Cooper lived with his biological mother who admitted to me that she hated Cooper. She told me that she hated men because of what they had done to her and that when she looked at Cooper all she could see was a "little man." I was unable to reach his mother well enough to get her to seek her own intervention and soon enough she stopped bringing Cooper for therapy.

Integration

My favorite illustration of the importance of integration comes from a remarkably effective reading program called *Lindamood-Bell* (Lindamood, Bell, & Lindamood, 1997). Many of the children I have worked with who experienced chronic stress or who have experienced one or more traumatic events were helped with their reading difficulties when they were asked to notice their sensations. They were instructed to become aware of what it felt like on the back of their teeth, their tongue, the roof of their mouth, and their lips when they made certain sounds as they decoded letter combinations and words. They were asked to notice whether they experienced tingling, vibration, or some other sensation as they read, and this engaged the part of their brain that was already highly activated by the stress and trauma of their lives.

The *Lindamood-Bell* approach to reading actually engages all three parts of the brain thus integrating and utilizing the *whole* brain in the learning process. The neocortex is engaged because children are learning to read words. The neocortex understands and responds to the language of words. The limbic brain is also engaged because children experience feelings while learning to read, like frustration when they aren't "getting it" or satisfaction when they do. The limbic brain is the part of the brain that understands and responds to feelings or emotions.

Most unique and effective for stressed and traumatized children, however, is the fact that the brain stem is also engaged in the learning process through the sensations they are helped to notice. Remember, the brain stem mediates the effects of stress and trauma. The brain stem is most activated and therefore most readily accessible to stressed and traumatized children. By communicating with the brain stem, we promote resonance with it, thereby soothing it and reintegrating it with the rest of the "triune" (or three-part) brain. The stressed and traumatized children that I referred to the program who had struggled for years learning to read and who were falling further and further behind improved their reading scores by two to three grade levels in a four week period.

When the whole person and the whole brain is communicated with and intervened with through sensations, the language of the brain stem, through feelings, the language of the limbic brain and through words, the language of the neocortex, integration and therefore coherence of all three parts of the brain is possible. SRT providers can help children notice and experience sensations, images, thoughts, behaviors, and emotions, connecting them all so that the full meaning and value of their experiences can be realized.

Integration of disconnected parts into a re-connected whole is what is most important for healing the effects of chronic stress and trauma. Different researchers and clinicians use different terms depending on their orientation, such as sensory integration or neural integration. The integration that is required for the resolution of chronic stress or trauma and the enhancement of self-regulatory capacity is all of these things and more. SRT intervenes to retrieve what was lost, a sense of wholeness and connection to self and others. By intervening at all levels, including the level of sensation and the brain stem, we re-integrate all of what it means to be human and all of what is required to learn and behave successfully as a member of society.

Psychoeducation and Support

An essential part of SRT is educating chronically stressed or traumatized children, when developmentally appropriate, as well as parents, educators, and anyone else working with our children about their unique needs. Understanding our children better *is* an intervention. With greater understanding, we become more willing to implement alternative more appropriate ways of responding and intervening. Psychoeducation, the more cognitive part of SRT, can never be left out of the process if it is to have long-term efficacy. Otherwise, the changes we work so hard to promote will not be maintained across settings. What SRT does to improve children's self-regulation can be undone when their unique needs continue to be misunderstood. Relationships can serve either to further engrain stress and trauma patterns in the brain or to promote the healthy resolution of such patterns. This is an essential message to disseminate.

14
When Should I Trust My Own Instincts?

Always! That is not to say we should not gather all the facts, examine all our options, hear what others have to say, including so-called experts in the field, but remember, we are the expert in knowing our children and their history. We may not have been raised to question authority, and our culture may teach us to value the opinion of people with letters on the end of their name, but we must remain cautious, even skeptical. Especially when someone suggests, recommends, or encourages the labeling or medicating of our children. There are now too many effective, alternative intervention options to be resigned to the observations and opinions of people who discourage us from the natural healing of our children. While it may be tempting at times to rely on others for answers to things we think we don't understand, we must remind ourselves that with enough investigation and persistence we can find sensible answers for our children that not only work but also let us sleep at night.

Shante

Shante was an eight-year-old third grade student who had been given a disciplinary transfer from one school to another due to repeated problems with teachers and administrators. Shante's mother, Ms. Brown, came to see me, wanting to do whatever she could to prevent any further disruptions to Shante's education.

When I met with Ms. Brown, she told me that her daughter began having behavior problems at the age of two. The problems were so great that she was "kicked out" of her YWCA play school. When she was three and four years of age, Shante had a "rough time" at the Child Development Center she attended. By first and second grade, Ms. Brown reported that Shante was doing "awful." She said that Shante could be doing "fine one minute, the next I don't know what's going on." Two to three times per week, Shante was "throwing tantrums" at home. Ms. Brown stated that, "minor things set her off big."

Shante had a "bad attitude," according to her new teacher. She was a "master manipulator" and used physical violence to get her way. Shante was described as defiant and stubborn on a daily basis. She was out of her seat "constantly" and often "glued" to another student in the class. If the teacher remained at her desk and stood "right there" beside Shante, she could stay in her seat and get her work done. Otherwise, she would avoid class work with psychosomatic complaints. The school nurse reported, for instance, that Shante made frequent visits to her office complaining of a sore head or upset tummy.

According to both Shante's teacher and babysitter, Shante liked to boss people around. She loved to be praised, hated to feel embarrassed, and engaged in "any power struggle to the end." The teacher also noted that if someone upset Shante, it was as if "the whole world had to come to an end."

I asked Ms. Brown whether or not Shante had ever experienced a fall, accident, injury, or hospitalization while growing up. Right away, Ms. Brown's face changed. She said, "No one has asked me that before.

Yes, something terrible happened. When Shante was two, she fell from the top bunk of a bunk bed and broke her elbow." Ms. Brown recounted the horror she experienced that day. She said she tried to put a coat on her daughter to be ready for transport to the hospital. When she tried to do so, Shante let out an excruciating scream. She looked down and saw that her two-year-old daughter's elbow was the "size of a lemon." Shante passed out from the pain. Ms. Brown shook her daughter trying to wake her but Shante would not stay conscious for more than seconds at a time. The fire department came and took them to the hospital. Ms. Brown reported that rather than the firemen being a powerful resource to her and her daughter, their conduct and demeanor made them feel more afraid than they already were.

I spoke with Ms. Brown about trauma and its impact on the nervous system. I let her know that it did not just happen to her daughter; it happened to her too. I helped her understand that she too may have unresolved trauma reactions that are easily triggered by minor events. She agreed stating that she knew exactly what I was talking about. I encouraged her to seek the support of her family and friends in trying to deal with her thoughts, feelings, and sensations related to what happened. I gave Ms. Brown a handout that would help her better understand her daughter and her daughter's needs as a traumatized child. She looked relieved to have this information and asked why no one had ever talked to her about this before.

Ms. Brown remembered one more incident she wanted to share with me. She said that when Shante was three or four years of age, she "went on a rage" and "attacked" another girl. She specifically remembered how hot Shante was, how much she was sweating, and how "full of rage" she was. She said she would never forget seeing her daughter that way. It was Shante's grandmother who was able to calm Shante down. She simply "held her and held her until [much later] Shante took a deep breath" and was calm again. I let Ms. Brown know that that was exactly the right thing to do and that she could also help Shante in the same way when the situation called for it. No unnecessary talking, no trying to stop the tears, just holding until that deep breath comes and the nervous system settles once again.

Ms. Brown went home with a better understanding of her daughter. The handout was something she could read at her own pace as many times as she needed in order to know how best to help Shante. I reassured her that I would work with Shante to help resolve the early trauma she had experienced. Before I did, I asked the teacher about Shante's resources and strengths and encouraged her to focus on these with Shante in class. She loved to sing and was a good reader. She liked to read aloud in front of the class. I asked the teacher to give Shante opportunities to do so.

I met with Shante three times on an individual basis. The first time I saw her, I picked her up from the nurse's office where she was complaining of the front of her head hurting. I brought her to my office and focused on building her internal resources through grounding and centering exercises. First, I had her stand in front of me and pretend, like me, that she was a tree. I directed her to feel her feet planted in the ground like roots of a tree connecting to the earth. I asked her to stretch her arms into the sky like branches reaching for the sunshine and swaying in the breeze. As we swayed back and forth like trees in the wind, strongly connected to the earth, I asked her what she noticed inside her body. She said her "tummy" was like a "giggly melon." "That's it," I said, "Just notice how your tummy feels like a giggly melon. Is that a pleasant feeling or an unpleasant feeling?" She smiled and said it was a "beautiful feeling."

As Shante and I stood face to face, after a few moments of allowing time for her to enjoy the "beautiful feeling," I taught her how to take full deep breaths. I took a deep breath in through my nose and filled my belly up with air. I had her watch my belly so she could see how it filled up when I inhaled. I held the breath for a few seconds and then let it out slowly through my mouth. Shante practiced a few and got better each time.

We moved to the table where I had her draw a picture of what it was like to be a tree planted in the ground with branches stretching up to the sunshine. She drew a picture of an apple tree with flowers and grass, sunshine and clouds, and a bird flying. I asked her where she felt something inside her body when she looked at the picture. She said her "tummy." I asked her what she felt there and she said it felt "smooth." I had her put her hand on her belly for a few minutes and asked her to attend to that smooth feeling. She left my office after about forty-five minutes, smiling and skipping.

I saw Shante six days later. I had her start by drawing a picture of something she was good at. She drew a picture of herself skipping rope. I had her look at the picture and notice what she felt inside her body. She said, "My tummy hurts." Within the context of resources, the unresolved effects of trauma can re-surface in order to be resolved. Shante was able to notice the unpleasant sensations in her tummy yet was not overwhelmed by them.

I asked her to tell me more about her tummy and how it hurt. "What does the hurt feel like?" I asked. "A rock," she answered. I asked for details about the rock to help her stay with what was happening in her stomach. "Does it have a color or a size?" "Yes," she said, "It's big and gray." "I see. It's big and gray," I said. "That's it. I'm right here with you...just notice how your tummy feels like there's a big gray rock inside." I allowed a few moments for Shante to be with the hurt in her tummy reminding her that I was right there with her. After a few moments, Shante's tummy still hurt so I asked her to remember how she was a tree with her feet planted in the ground. I reminded her of the sunshine on her face. Then I asked her what else she noticed in her body. She said she felt "strong." I asked her where and she said in her "legs." "That's it," I said, "Notice how strong you feel in your legs." I allowed time for her to be with that feeling. When I asked her again about the rock in her stomach, she said it was much smaller and did not hurt as much.

After a few moments, I gave Shante a picture of a silhouette of a body and asked her to color in the silhouette with different colors that corresponded with different sensations she noticed in the present moment. She felt "soft" in her head and face and "flowing" in her tummy with the exception of one small black circle that she drew in the center of her stomach. The "gray rock" was still there but it was now very small. I did some deep breathing with Shante for a few moments and then had her draw another picture. This time it was a picture of how she liked to be comforted. Shante drew a picture of two things. She drew herself at home taking a bath, and then one of her vacuuming. I reminded Shante of how she could take deep breaths in class or on the playground before she got upset and how she could remember her roots planted in the earth with the sun shining on her face.

Four days later I checked with the nurse who reported that Shante was doing "much better" and not going to her office as frequently. After another five days, I learned from the teacher that the main residual issue was defiance. The mother was helping with that, however, and it was getting better. I saw Shante one last time.

Shante and I reviewed the grounding and breathing exercises we had done together before. She drew a picture of a happy time in her life. She drew herself playing ball with a friend. I had Shante look at the picture she drew and notice what she felt inside her body as she looked at it. Then I gave her a silhouette and asked her to color in what she felt inside. She drew orange on her face and head, reporting that she felt warm there. I allowed time for Shante to feel into her sensations and as she did, something very important happened. Her head started to move back and forth slowly and her eyes began rolling into the back of her head. I did not interrupt what was happening. I simply stated quietly, "That's it, Shante. I'm right here with you."

As I watched Shante's head move very specifically, I was struck with a sense that this was how her head and eyes must have moved when she went in and out of consciousness during the accident. Although she remained conscious and seated at the table, after a few moments of Shante looking like she could pass out, she yawned widely. I kept my hand on her upper mid-back and said, "That's it. You're doing great, Shante." She took several short breaths and then one large deep breath seemed to take her. She became more alert and oriented back to the room. I asked her if she was doing okay. She said yes. I had her rest a few moments. Then I reviewed with her all the beautiful pictures she drew and acknowledged her hard work. I told her she could come back and see me anytime.

Shante stopped going to the nurse's office completely. I referred her and her mother to a community agency to help with some of the bad habits that had been formed over the years they struggled to understand the situation. It took a while for those services to commence but in the meantime, Shante did not report any more psychosomatic complaints and was doing much better in class and on the playground. Well over a year after Shante and I worked together, the nurse remarked what a different girl she was. She said that Shante had become a pleasure to talk with and be around. The community agency involved with Shante and her mother reported that, after a year of counseling involving play and art therapy, their services were being decreased due to excellent progress.

Shante was a child who had been well on her way to becoming identified for special education as a student with "emotional disturbance." She had a history of behavior problems commencing at the age of two that had been resistant to the interventions commonly put into place for "difficult" children. Parent conferences were held at the play school, the Child Development Center, and Shante's schools when she was in Kindergarten and first grade. She was put on behavior contracts and counseled by her teachers and school counselors. She was given "fresh starts" at new schools. Without taking a history of trauma with the mother, however, the "experts" that Ms. Brown relied upon did not know how to intervene in the best way possible. They did not understand who Shante was and what her specific needs were. One meeting with the parent, one meeting with the teacher, and three individual sessions with Shante helped turn her life around. The support of counseling from a commu-

nity agency assisted Shante not only in maintaining her physiological gains of a more balanced nervous system but also in achieving the additional goal of decreasing defiance.

Now that you know the signs and symptoms of chronic stress and trauma in your child, as well as how chronic stress and trauma affect the brain and nervous system, you are the expert in your struggling child's life. You know your child's history, spirit, and how he or she has been changed by what happened or is happening still. You now know the best ways to intervene with your stressed or traumatized child. Going forward, don't just follow the steps outlined in this book, share them with doctors, nurses, dentists, teachers, principals, and anyone else that works with your child and wants to tell you what the problem is and how to intervene. Informed by your new knowledge, you won't be taken down the wrong path of intervention no matter how sophisticated and impressive that path may seem, not when you trust your instincts.

Your instincts are the gift of the oldest part of your brain, the brain stem, the part of you that is solely focused on survival. Not just your survival but survival of the species. When the brain stem speaks to you through its language of sensations, through the "pit" you feel in your stomach – the "gut feeling" you sense deep inside of you about right and wrong – it is to guide you to do what will aid in the survival of your child. When you take care of yourself with resources that keep you in your optimum zone of arousal, self-regulating stress in a healthy way, you are able to notice the sensations of your body and use them as signals that communicate to you what is right and what isn't. Start there and you will see *you can heal your child.*

Conclusion

When we recognize the signs and symptoms of chronic stress or trauma in our children we can begin the process of healing. As we now know, healing is possible when we communicate through the language of sensations with the parts of the brain most involved in, and affected by, stress and trauma. Stressful and traumatic events are experienced and recalled not just by our cognitive mind but also by our brain and body. The longer we engage only the cognitive mind in the healing process, which is what we do when we send our stressed or traumatized child to an anger management group or to a traditional talk therapist, the longer healing does not take place – especially not in the long term. In fact, such approaches, although helpful with other kinds of problems, have the potential to *increase* suffering in the chronically stressed or traumatized child.

The new insights that come from cognitive approaches without the body's capacity to follow through can set up our troubled children for feelings of greater failure, shame, and helplessness. We often say, "When we know better, we do better," but that simply isn't true for stressed and traumatized children. Increased suffering is inevitable when cognitive approaches like anger management teach our children better ways of behaving - so they now *know* better – but don't intervene with the part of them that will support them in *doing* better – their nervous system. No matter what their cognitive mind thinks is possible, their body has not been engaged in the healing process and, therefore, has not been helped to physically tolerate the feelings and sensations of pain and discomfort that their daily lives evoke. It is through the building of the specific kinds of resources discussed in this book, as well as Self-Regulation Therapy, that the body's natural ability to self-regulate all sensations and feelings, good and bad, is restored so that tolerance and joy are not only possible, they're automatic.

Additional Resources

Books

Aldort, N. (2006). *Raising Our Children, Raising Ourselves: Transforming Parent-Child Relationships from Reaction and Struggle to Freedom, Power, and Joy.* Bothell, WA: Book Publishers Network.

Gendlin, E.T. (1981). *Focusing.* New York: Bantam Books.

Lawlis, F. (2005). *The ADD Answer: How to Help Your Child Now.* New York: Plume.

Levine, P.A. (1997). *Waking the Tiger: Healing Trauma.* Berkeley: North Atlantic Books.

Levine, P.A. & Kline, M. (2008). *Trauma-Proofing Your Child: A Parent's Guide for Instilling Confidence, Joy, and Resilience.* Berkeley: North Atlantic Books.

Levine, P.A. & Kline, M. (2006). *Trauma through a Child's Eyes: Awakening the Ordinary Miracle of Healing.* Berkeley: North Atlantic Books.

Melrose, R. (2006). *Why Students Underachieve: What Educators and Parents Can Do about It.* Lanham, Maryland: Rowman & Littlefield Education.

Melrose, R. (2006). *Hope and Healing: An Activities Book for Adults Working with School-Aged Children.* San Francisco: 60 Seconds Press.

Melrose, R. (2006). *Hope and Healing: A Guide for Parents of Traumatized Children.* Self-published (available only at DrMelrose. com).

Terr, L. (1990). *Too Scared to Cry: How Trauma Affects Children and Ultimately Us All.* New York: Basic Books.

Williams, M.S. & Shellenberger, S. (2001). *Take Five! Staying Alert at Home and School.* Albuquerque, NM: Therapy Works, Inc.

Audio

Levine, P.A. (2001). *It Won't Hurt Forever: Guiding Your Child Through Trauma*. Louisville, CO: Sounds True.

Websites

(Most of the following websites will help you find a brain or body-based trauma healing practitioner in your area.)

AlertProgram.com

AuthenticParent.com

aapb.org (The Association for Applied Psychophysiology and Biofeedback)

cftre.com (The Canadian Foundation for Trauma Research and Education)

DrMelrose.com

HealingResources.info

NaomiAldort.com

SensorimotorPsychotherapy.org

SomaticExperiencing.com

TraumaHealing.com

References

Bremmer, J.D., Krystal, J.H., Charnez, D.S., & Southwick, S.M. (1996). Neural mechanisms in dissociative amnesia for childhood abuse: Relevance to the current controversy surrounding false memory syndrome. *American Journal of Psychiatry,* 153, 71-80.

Dacey, J. S., and L. B. Fiore. 2002. *Your anxious child: How parents and teachers can relieve anxiety in children.* San Francisco: Jossey-Bass.

Gendlin, E. T. 1981. *Focusing.* New York: Bantam Books.

Gillis, S. 2003. Autogenics visualization. At http://www.trigenics. net/journals/StevegGillis-AutogenicVisualization.htm.

Heegaard, M. 1993. *When something terrible happens: Children can learn to cope with grief.* Minneapolis, Minn.: Woodland Press.

Levine, P. A. 1997. *Waking the tiger: Healing trauma.* Berkeley: North Atlantic Books.

————. 2003. *Tools for times of terror and turbulence: A body-based approach to trauma treatment.* A professional talk at the University of San Diego, February.

Lindamood, P., N. Bell, and P. Lindamood. 1997. Sensory-cognitive factors in the controversy over reading instruction. *Journal of Developmental and Learning Disorders* 1:143–82.

Oaklander, V. 1988. *Windows to our children.* New York: The Gestalt Journal Press.

O'Neill, C. 1993. *Relax.* Toronto: Child's Play (International).

Perry, B.D., Pollard, R.A., Blakley, T.L., Baker, W.L., & Vigilante, D. (1995). Childhood trauma, the neurobiology of adaptation, and "use-dependent" development of the brain: How "states" become "traits." *Infant Mental Health,* 16, 271-291.

Schore, A.N. 1994. *Affect regulation and the origin of the self.* Hillsdale, N.J.: Lawrence Erlbaum.

————. 1998. Early shame experience and the development of the infant brain. In *Shame, interpersonal behavior, psychopathology, and culture,* edited by P. Gilbert and B. Andrews, 57–77. London: Oxford University Press.

————. 2003. *Affect regulation and repair of the self.* R. Cassidy Seminars. Santa Rosa, Calif.: R. Cassidy Seminars.

Siegel, D. (2003). *Attachment and self-understanding: Parenting with the brain in mind.* FACES: A National Conference, Mastering Counseling with the Masters, San Diego, October.

Starknum, M.N., Gebarski, S.S., Berent, S., & Schterngart, D.E. (1992). Hippocampal formation volume, memory of dysfunction, and cortisol levels in patients with Cushing's Syndrome. *Biology Psychiatry,* 32, 756-765.

Steele, W., & Raider, M. (2001). *Structured sensory interventions for children, adolescents, and parents.* New York: Edwin Mellen Press.

Stroufe, A. 1996. *Emotional development: The organization of emotional life in the early years.* New York: Cambridge University Press.

Teicher, M. (2000). The neurobiology of child abuse. *Scientific American,* 68-75.

van der Kolk, B.A. (2002). *The effects of trauma on the self: The aftermath of terror.* FACES: A National Conference, Mastering Counseling with the Masters, San Diego, November.

Wissel, H. 1994. Shooting: A state of mind. *Scholastic Coach* (January).

Yang, B., & Clum, G.A. (2000). Childhood stress leads to later suicidality via its effects on cognitive functioning. *Suicide and Life Threatening Behavior,* 30, 83-189.

About the Author

Dr. Regalena "Reggie" Melrose is an adjunct professor at California State University, Long Beach, as well as a licensed clinical and credentialed school psychologist. She worked in public schools for thirteen years with children of all ages (and their families) in a variety of roles: as a school psychologist, district-wide coordinator of mental health services, lead psychologist for elementary schools, and member of the task force for children with emotional disturbance. She wrote a book based on her experiences entitled, *Why Students Underachieve: What Educators and Parents Can Do about It* (Rowman & Littlefield, 2006), to help educators know how to increase achievement and success in their most baffling and challenging students. Dr. Melrose created adjunct booklets full of tools and resources for parents, educators, and others to accompany her book. The booklets are called, *Hope and Healing: An Activities Book for Adults Working with School-Aged Children* (60 Seconds Press, 2009) and, *Hope and Healing: A Guide for Parents of Traumatized Children* (Melrose, 2006).

Dr. Melrose opened a private practice as a trauma healing specialist and Somatic Experiencing Practitioner (SEP) in the year 2001 and maintains that practice today. She is an international speaker currently providing education and training to school districts, medical and mental health professionals, as well as parent groups. She accepts inquiries for all her services at DrMelrose.com.

Other books & resources by Dr. Melrose...

Why Students Underachieve:

What Educators and Parents Can Do about It

Rowman & Littlefield, 2006, ISBN-13: 978-1578864409

A 220-page textbook designed for all educators (teachers, administrators, and school support personnel) to easily access real stories of traumatized students in order to understand them, what they look like in the classroom and on the playground, and what their particular needs are. The book is full of personal stories, case examples, and most importantly, effective and easy-to-use tools that can be implemented immediately with traumatized students in order to first, do no harm, and second, provide them with a real chance for a promising future.

Hope & Healing:

An Activities Book for Adults Working with School-Aged Children

60 Seconds Press, 2006 • ISBN 13: 978-0-615-89099-9

A practical and easily accessible guide for any adult working with children who have suffered through trauma, tragedy or loss. It is the precise book I was searching for when I was working with so many troubled children who needed very specific kinds of therapeutic activities in order to heal from their experiences. Parents, teachers, and counselors or therapists of any kind can use the numerous activities in this book with individual children, or with groups of children, to help them tap into their resources, strengths, and resiliencies. Once the first book is read, the importance of completing the activities in the second book is clearly understood. The effectiveness of the ideas and recommendations in the second book would likely be compromised without referring back to the information in the first book where all of the activities are explained in greater detail and with examples.

Hope & Healing:

A Guide for Parents of Traumatized Children

60 Seconds Press, 2006 • EN: ISBN 978-0-615-88569-8
SP: ISBN 978-0-9912953-2-6

A 25-page booklet for parents of traumatized children. Available in English and Spanish, this guide simply explains what trauma is, what it can look like in children at home and at school, and what parents or guardians can do to facilitate healing. The booklet is a perfect hand-out for school counseling and nursing offices.

To find out about exciting training possibilities with Dr. Melrose, contact her by visiting her website, DrMelrose.com

Made in the USA
San Bernardino, CA
13 September 2016